PHYLIS SAVARI

RESTORING BALANCE IN THE AGE OF ALGORITHMS

CONTENTS

Thank you to Rebecca Holland for generously donating the cover
image, entitled *The Path*. To view more of Ms. Holland's stunning oil
paintings, please visit www.rebeccaholland.online or the Coastal
Arts League Gallery in Half Moon Bay, California.

To my mentor, MaryAnn,
for her generosity and steadfast light

PREFACE

Dear Reader,

It took a relatively short time for me to realize that my data science career in Silicon Valley was harmful to my well-being and that the industry prioritized profit over people. On the other hand, it took many years for me to overcome the effects and spread the message that every one of us can use data to bring more joy into the world. I hope that sharing my story will help you navigate technology with greater power and purpose.

This book based on my personal experiences and research. I haven't mentioned names, other than those of public figures, to protect everyone's privacy.

CHAPTER 1
AWARENESS

When the World Wide Web opened to the public in 1991, it didn't make international headlines. It didn't even make headlines at the Massachusetts Institute of Technology (MIT), where I was an undergraduate student in electrical engineering at the time.

The first website (http://info.cern.ch) was published by the inventor of "the web," Tim Berners-Lee, and was aptly about the World Wide Web (W3) project. He described it as "a wide-area hypermedia information retrieval initiative aiming to give universal access to a large universe of documents."[1] A marketer would have announced the birth of the web with a bit more pizzazz and fanfare, but the unassuming, functional description was written by an engineer for engineers. Berners-Lee created the project at the Conseil Européen pour la Recherche Nucléaire (CERN) to make it easier to share documents for CERN's thousands of researchers across the globe using different computer systems.

Basically, the W3 project simplified sharing via the internet, providing technology standards and software for publishing and accessing information. The stroke of genius was linking one page to others to create an interconnected web of information. For end users, this meant one could "surf" from one page to the next simply by clicking links.

By the end of 1991, only a handful of websites had been published. By the end of 1992, a few dozen websites existed, mainly created by universities and research labs. In 1993, a user-friendly web browser, Mosaic, made the web more easily accessible to PC and Mac users. That same year, MIT's student-run newspaper, *The Tech*, became the first publication to deliver content on the web. By the end of 1993, there were more than 600 websites and the web accounted for 1 percent of internet traffic.

I remember using Mosaic in 1993 to browse the web while I was a master's student in operations research at Stanford University. I felt both amazed and overwhelmed by the sheer weight of information and how quickly it was being updated. My university courses still used hard-copy textbooks and reference materials. When I needed to download a research paper over the internet, I used the file transfer protocol (FTP) process, which typically took several minutes. Downloading related documents involved repeating the FTP process, provided I was lucky enough to get a hold of the access details, or checking the school library to see if the papers were available on microfilm. On the web, however, all I needed was the web address (URL) of the research paper to access not only the paper but all its linked documents, all the linked documents' linked documents, and so on, saving countless hours of FTPing and library searches.

When it came to exploring the web, I learned about new websites through word of mouth. If I was looking for a specific piece of information, I typed the URL of the most relevant website that I knew of into Mosaic. I started to click links that seemed most likely to bring me closer to what I was looking for. If I seemed to be moving farther away, I backtracked and headed down another path. It was like playing a game of hot and cold. As the number of websites increased, it became more like finding a needle in the haystack.

Then, in 1994, the web really began to take flight.

Berners-Lee left CERN for MIT, where he founded the International World Wide Web Consortium (W3C) to create open standards for the web. The basis for the standards was royalty-free technology, enabling widespread adoption.

Search engines such as Lycos (founded at Carnegie Mellon), Webcrawler (founded at University of Washington), and World Wide Web Worm (founded at University of Colorado) were released to help end users find the most relevant web pages for their topic of interest. Like today, one only needed to know the URL of a search engine website, type a phrase into a search box, and then the engine would return a ranked list of relevant pages generated by an algorithm (a "step-by-step procedure for solving a problem"[2]). Early search engine algorithms generally ranked pages based on how many times a search phrase appeared on a page. While the concept of a search engine was groundbreaking and foundational to web adoption, the initial technology was rudimentary and lacked the quality and speed we're used to today.

Stanford graduate students Jerry Yang and David Filo decided to use a different approach to help end users navigate the web. In 1994 they released *Jerry and David's Guide to the World Wide Web*, a human-curated directory of websites by category, akin to a *Yellow Pages* for the internet. They also featured lists such as "What's New?" and "What's Cool?" to help people discover new, interesting websites. This high-quality, engaging, and relatively fast solution quickly hooked me in.

By the end of 1994, more than 10,000 websites had been published, 18 percent of which had commercial ("dot-com") web addresses,[3] with an estimated 10 million global web users (approximately 0.2 percent of the world's population).[4] The White House had a website, Pizza Hut started selling pizzas over the web, and the website name sex.com was registered. The technology race was on, especially with search engines that could still deliver high-quality results even with the exponentially increasing number of websites and end users performing searches. Advertising as a revenue model for websites also began in 1994, enabling free content and applications on much of the web.

Yang and Filo rebranded their website in 1995 and officially founded Yahoo!, which stood for Yet Another Hierarchical Officious Oracle, referring to its hierarchical directory. They also added Yahoo! Search, which was a search performed on the Yahoo! Directory rather than the text of web pages as a search engine did. Unlike many dot-com startups, the first chief executive officer (CEO) of Yahoo! was not one of the founders. Instead, someone with leadership experience was selected. Tim Koogle, a former Motorola executive and Stanford alum, was chosen while Yang and Filo each took on the title Chief Yahoo!.

During this time, I was working in financial services, doing what is referred to today as "data science": the discipline of extracting insights from data (quantitative and qualitative) to drive decisions and achieve goals. We all consume and analyze data to guide our choices. Everyday "data-driven decisions" include assessing nutrition labels and checking prices when choosing what items to buy at the supermarket, reading reviews and watching trailers when picking a movie, reviewing your bank account balance when planning for a big purchase, and checking in with your body when determining what type of self-care to do. Corporations do the same thing on a larger scale by using hardware and software under the supervision of data engineers and analysts.

In my financial services jobs, I built statistical models that, for example, predicted the likelihood of a consumer applying for financial products or created driving routes for armored trucks maintaining automated teller machines (ATMs).

In the mid-1990s, there were relatively few data insights jobs in dot-com and other technology startups. The greatest need was for computer scientists and software engineers. In addition, technology startups tended to have long hours for relatively low pay. They lured people with generous stock options that could potentially make you rich enough to retire if the company had a successful initial public offering (IPO). It was a high-risk, high-reward situation, often compared with the mid-1800s gold rush in North America. I knew a few people who earned millions, some who earned hundreds of thousands but were not satisfied, and others who went bust.

As someone who valued work-life balance and had student loans to repay, this employment model didn't work for me. But I kept browsing dot-com job listings because I knew I wanted to work in the quickly evolving web industry. Eventually, I found an online technology information publisher, ZDNet, that advertised a thirty-five-hour workweek. They offered higher pay than I was making in financial services and they were at the forefront of using data to personalize website content.

The team had just built a data warehouse (a repository of data) of all the pages viewed for each visitor to the website. I was hired as the first data analyst to explore and gather insights from this data. My first project was to segment visitors based on their website activity so that on their next visit they would be served a customized version of the homepage. For example, a segment of users who came to the website primarily for gaming news would have more gaming content on their homepage than on the default page. These tailored homepages would be created based on the activity profiles of each segment and the editor's own content selection process. I was very excited to be part of this work, which was cutting edge at the time.

Shortly after I had completed my first pass at the algorithm for segmenting users, the company was acquired by its main competitor, CNET. It was estimated that the combined website would have more than 16 million visitors a month, which would be the eighth highest on the web.[5]

The merger overlapped with the 2000 dot-com crash, and I witnessed my first round of tech layoffs. I was told that CNET wanted a brand-new data warehouse built for the merged website, similar to the one that had been built by ZDNet. If I wanted to work on building the new data warehouse, I could stay. Otherwise, I would be laid off because a data analyst was no longer needed. I chose to stay, even though it wasn't work that I enjoyed. I was very glad I did.

Working on the new data warehouse turned out to be critical training for my data career and a huge gift. I learned where the data I analyzed came from and could trace each action a visitor took on the website all the way through the "data pipeline" (the series of steps for collecting, storing, processing, and delivering data) to a metric in a report.

While I was disappointed that my algorithm never saw the light of day due to the acquisition, It still helped me to understand the purpose and nuances of each step in the data pipeline and where my new role of data processing fit in. As my understanding of the data pipeline grew, I noticed parallels to the food industry and the farm-to-fork pipeline (see Table 1).

Serving Personalized Farm-to-Fork Meal	Serving Personalized ZDNet Homepage Content in 2000 (Proposed)
U-pick farm created	Website created
Crops planted by farm workers	Content written by staff writers
Crops harvested by U-pick farm customer	Content viewed by website visitor
Customer's harvest tagged and packaged	Visitor's activity details logged and packaged
Harvest containers transported to food warehouse	Activity logs imported into data warehouse
Ingredients processed: sorted, cleaned, and prepped	Data processed: sorted, cleaned, and prepped
Recipe created by recipe developer from processed ingredients	Algorithm created by data analyst from processed data
Personalized farm-to-fork meal prepared by chef based on recipe and professional judgment	Personalized homepage prepared by editor based on algorithm results and professional judgment
Personalized farm-to-fork meal served to U-pickcustomer	Personalized homepage content served to website visitor

Table 1. Comparing the Data Pipeline to the Food Pipeline

In 2000, I had taken for granted that editors chose the content on the ZDNet homepage and that the output of my segmentation algorithm would have been only one factor in their decision-making process. In my opinion, it struck a good balance between art and science, with a human as the master and a machine as the servant. I never imagined that in the future some websites would eliminate editors from the content selection process and rely solely on algorithms. They would also source their content from a mix of verified and unverified sources. Web content consumption would go from a mainstream, restaurant-like experience to an outré potluck with some dishes prepared by master chefs and others by mass murderers. A computer would decide what combination to serve a visitor.

I also took for granted other aspects of my first dot-com job. One was the company culture, which was open and exploratory. My first boss had an anthropology degree, my second boss had a music degree, the engineering whiz on our team didn't have a degree and had started at the company doing data entry, the receptionist was learning html, and two colleagues on other teams had apprenticed with Ansel Adams! We worked together to help each other succeed. My boss took the time to understand each of our work styles and supported us accordingly. These days, talented individuals like these would likely be passed over due to ageism, lack of a technology degree, and/or valuing employee satisfaction too highly.

After working on the data pipeline for more than four years, I longed to analyze data again, so I resigned. My boss connected me with a former co-worker of ours who was part of the business intelligence team for Yahoo! Media Group, which included Yahoo! News, Yahoo! Sports, and Yahoo! Finance. She referred me to the business intelligence engineering team for a role, and after several interviews I received a job offer. I would be processing and analyzing data to provide product performance insights and, as was common industry practice, 20 percent of my time would be designated for exploration and creating my own projects. That sounded wonderful to me.

I was incredibly grateful to receive this job offer. When I joined Yahoo! in 2006, it had the highest page views on the web, averaging 3.8 billion a day from nearly 500 million monthly visitors across the globe.[6] This was 70 percent of monthly internet users and 14 percent of the world population aged fifteen and older.[7] While these were impressive statistics,

I was more drawn to the underlying dynamics of Yahoo!'s role in the evolution of the web.

In the ten years since going public, Yahoo! had stopped categorizing websites like they used to – the number of websites became prohibitively high. To maintain their dominance in the industry, they embraced algorithmic search engines through various partnerships as the technology kept evolving. In 1996 they made a deal with AltaVista (founded at Digital Equipment Corporation in Palo Alto), and in 1998 they made a deal with Inktomi (founded at University of California, Berkeley.)

Also in 1998, two Stanford PhD students, Larry Page and Sergey Brin, filed a patent for their PageRank search algorithm, which ranked relevance by the number and quality of links to a page rather than counting the number of times a search term appeared on the page. Page and Brin offered Yahoo! the opportunity to buy the technology for $1 million, but they were rejected. They went on to receive other funding and founded Google that year.

In 2000, Yahoo! struck a deal with Google to power its searches. Two years later, the new Yahoo! CEO, Terry Semel, tried to acquire Google for $3 billion, but they countered with $5 billion and a deal was never reached. Instead, Yahoo! acquired their previous search engine partner, Inktomi, and then Overture Services, which owned Yahoo!'s first search engine partner, AltaVista. Based on these acquisitions, Yahoo! developed its own search engine technology and stopped using Google to power searches in 2004. Google became viewed more as a competitor than a partner.

By the time I joined Yahoo!, Google Search was the top search site on the web and growing. Yahoo! Search was second and trying to keep up. Even I used Google Search because it was faster and the results were better.

The first generation of the web, Web 1.0, was about simplifying information access. Arguably, the two most important end-user tools for facilitating this were the web browser and search engine, giving Google the upper hand over Yahoo!.

Yahoo!, however, was differentiating itself from Google with Web 2.0 experiences. Web 2.0 was about user interactivity, including the opportunity for users to create content and connect with each other. Yahoo!'s photo-sharing website, Flickr (acquired in 2005), was an acclaimed example. Yahoo! Answers was a community-driven site for Q&A. Yahoo! Music allowed users to share playlists with one another. The division I was in experimented with interactive content such as *The 9*, a daily video show hosted by Maria Sansone in which users could click on, vote for, and submit top finds on the web. *The 9* was a modern take on the "What's New?" and "What's Cool?" lists from *Jerry and David's Guide to the Web*. Most of these ideas were overtaken by competitors years later, but in early 2006 Yahoo! was paving the way for innovative web experiences.

Google and Yahoo! also had strikingly different user-interface styles. Google's homepage was primarily whitespace with the main focus being the search box. Yahoo!'s homepage was a web portal, with a search box at the top and a newspaper-like layout below with sections on the weather, email access, sports, horoscopes, and so on. It also included ads, while Google's homepage did not. Yahoo!'s main competitor as a web portal was Microsoft, which had the largest audience on the web and the third-highest page views.

Life on the Yahoo! campus reflected the company's success, playful culture, and overwhelmingly young male employee base. The headquarters was a nerdtopia of game rooms, free lattes, purple cows, nap rooms, and beach volleyball courts. There was often live entertainment, including a performance outside the cafeteria by a seventeen-year-old Taylor Swift!

During my interviews, the team mentioned that Earth, Wind, and Fire had just played at the company's holiday party. Another day saw an exhibition game by the foosball world champions after their win in Las Vegas. I didn't know competitive foosball existed and found it captivating to watch. Like many tech companies, Yahoo! went all out for Oktoberfest with annual company beer mugs, live polka music, and yodelers. A few years earlier, Yahoo! had set the Guinness World Record for the largest simultaneous yodel.

One of the most important cultural facets for me was that Yahoo! wanted employees to stay for many years. During my interview process, I was told that employees received a gumball machine at five years of service, an espresso machine at ten years, and a foosball table at fifteen years. Nobody had received a foosball table yet since the company was only about a decade old, but they had already planned for the milestone. The thought of having a foosball table in the middle of my living room didn't exactly fill me with joy, but I appreciated the sense of job security.

The flip side was that employees were expected to "bleed purple" (purple was the company color), which meant having blind loyalty to Yahoo!'s products and "evangelizing" them to friends and family. Many employees had a cult-like zeal for the company. A couple even drove purple cars with vehicle-sized Yahoo! logos. I had used a Gmail address on my résumé and was told later that it could have automatically disqualified me. It genuinely hadn't occurred to me that it would be a problem; I only realized the magnitude of my error after it was pointed out.

Was I proud to work at Yahoo!? Yes. Was I preach-Yahoo-to-others and drive-a-purple-Yahoo-mobile proud? No. Fortunately, my teammates had a similar outlook and were dedicated, yet grounded and objective. They also bought lottery tickets every week and I joined in. As much as we enjoyed working at Yahoo!, not working at all was more appealing to most of us.

One of my early projects was a cost/benefit analysis of a Yahoo! Media Group news site reporting from major war zones around the world. It got a lot of visitors and was highly acclaimed by the press. Unfortunately, the advertising revenue didn't offset the production costs. People new to Yahoo! who came for the original content tended not to explore other parts of Yahoo! or return. Yahoo! was ahead of its time with the original content it produced, but in 2006 the only competitive option was to provide it to users for free, which was unsustainable.

An ongoing part of my job was to analyze A/B tests, also known as bucket tests, a common and integral part of data science and data-driven product design. An A/B test splits consumers into two or more groups, each experiencing a different version of a web page or other product feature. The performance of the two groups is then compared using a variety of metrics to measure success, such as page views and time spent, and whichever version has the best results is implemented. The first test I analyzed was on Yahoo! Games. One of the product managers wanted to test different lengths of time for the free trial period of a new Windows game called *Pirate Poppers* to see which resulted in the highest "conversion rate" (percentage of trial users who purchased the game).

As I settled into my day-to-day role, one issue came up quickly. The volume of data that Yahoo! was collecting was so large it wasn't viable to use traditional data warehousing products such as Oracle. In addition to the 3.8 billion page views per day, Yahoo! also tracked link clicks, advertising impressions, and other activity, easily surpassing 10 billion events per day. To give some context using a business in the physical world, McDonald's was processing "merely" tens of millions of transactions per day. This meant that my team had to work with small samples of raw log files that we processed ourselves for each analysis.

Lacking tools which could handle the huge amount of data was an industry-wide problem. The quest for "big data" technology began years earlier in conjunction with the web search engine race. The web had grown to 80 million sites[8] and 700 million monthly visitors,[9] with both figures increasing rapidly. It was vital for search engines to maintain their performance levels while cost-effectively scaling for continued growth.

The month I joined Yahoo!, the solution arrived. Yahoo! released Hadoop, a revolutionary open-source software technology that enabled data storage and processing to be "distributed" across computers which could be added or removed as needed. For example, if the volume of data doubled, doubling the number of computers would keep the processing time the same at double the cost. In short, Hadoop could process high volumes of data quickly and inexpensively. One of the tradeoffs was that Hadoop didn't meet the transaction compliance standards that products like Oracle enforced. These standards were necessary for financial transactions but were overkill for data applications on the web.

Hadoop was co-founded by Doug Cutting and Mike Cafarella, and much of the underlying research occurred when Cutting worked at Google. In 2006, he joined Yahoo! Search to help with its search engine performance and started the Hadoop project, which he named after his son's toy elephant. This was part of Yahoo! Search's efforts to catch up with Google Search. Hadoop was quickly adopted by several Silicon Valley companies, such as IBM and Facebook. However, it took time for it to be adopted more broadly in the industry and in other Yahoo! departments because it required specialized engineering training. Over the next few years, training became more widely available and solutions for simplifying or outsourcing complexities emerged.

Another big data technology breakthrough in 2006 was the release of Amazon Web Services (AWS). It offered "cloud computing," which is on-demand data storage and computing over the internet (the internet is typically represented with a cloud icon in engineering diagrams). Large tech companies built and managed their own data centers, but it was not feasible for smaller companies to do so. AWS made it possible for businesses of all sizes to quickly and inexpensively ramp up their data storage and processing needs, a prerequisite for using Hadoop.

The combination of Hadoop and AWS was a quantum leap for big data and, in my opinion, opened the gateway to "the age of algorithms." It would become standard practice for websites to integrate algorithms into their consumer experiences, personalizing both content and advertising. Big data applications would further expand into other industries, such as healthcare and agriculture.

As significant as all this was, even more momentous developments were to come in 2006. The lay of the land of the World Wide Web was shifting enormously. Like massive tectonic plates colliding, deflecting, and sliding past one another, the tech giants were in the process of forming the mountains and oceans of the online world.

In June, Yahoo! offered to purchase social media rising star Facebook for $1 billion, but owner Mark Zuckerberg declined. He was twenty-two years old and Facebook had fewer than 10 million users as it was mainly focused on college students.[10] Yahoo! also offered to buy YouTube for an undisclosed amount but lost out to Google, which purchased it for $1.65 billion in October. YouTube was an unprofitable startup of sixty-seven employees but was tremendously popular. The next generation of web leaders had rejected Yahoo!, from which the company never recovered. The truth was that Yahoo! was chasing the success of others more than they were leading the way on the web.

Perhaps the biggest web upheaval came in September when Facebook released its News Feed. Prior to its launch, Facebook users had to surf from one friend's page to the next to check for updates, Web 1.0-style. The News Feed eliminated this step. An algorithm would do the surfing for the user and present a consolidated list of updates across all their friends, Web 2.0-style. Initially, the algorithm sorted the updates in chronological order.

This was a big deal for a number of reasons. For one, it formally established users' lives as "news" and users as news contributors, which brought with it a certain responsibility to oneself and one's readers when submitting profile updates. What would you contribute to your friends' smorgasbord of news? And how often did you want to "feed" them a morsel of your life? A more consequential impact was that online socializing was now being orchestrated by an algorithm instead of by the users themselves, with the goal of being more efficient. The original process of visiting friends' profiles one by one to see what they'd been up to better mimicked real-life relationship dynamics. The News Feed, however, was far more convenient – a bit like making a call instead of seeing someone in person. Over time, Facebook's algorithm would evolve to use artificial intelligence (AI) to decide how to sort the News Feed, with the goal of maximizing engagement.

There was an immediate backlash from users. Not everyone wanted to be an extreme extrovert, broadcasting every change of their profile. Facebook responded with: "We didn't take away any privacy options."[11] The News Feed was here to stay, establishing a new content creation and consumption model for the web.

As a private person, I was glad I didn't have a Facebook account. I also found that I wasn't drawn to YouTube and other popular Web 2.0 experiences. I could understand the appeal of these powerful platforms and sensed that something huge would emerge from them, but I didn't feel the same pull as with Web 1.0. Some part of me wanted to run away from Silicon Valley, but another part of me knew it would be quite an experience to witness the "web-volution" up close. I liked my team and my projects and I didn't have anywhere to go, so I stayed.

Looking at the bigger picture, innovative young men with a desire to connect humanity had created a new, online world. From its conception in 1989 by Tim-Berners Lee to the pivotal events in 2006, extraordinary progress had been made. It felt as if the equivalent of hundreds of millions of years of evolution on Earth had been compressed into just seventeen years on the web! This rapid growth was happening without any internal and external checks and balances. The lack of diversity, femininity, wisdom, life experience, and legal accountability in the development of the web would take a toll on the inner dynamics of web companies, the products they created, the users who consumed them, the non-users who interacted with them, and the outside observers who wondered what was going on.

By the end of 2006, the head of Yahoo! Media Group left. Morale had declined and the company pulled back on extravagances like live music and festivities. In June 2007, CEO Terry Semel stepped down, replaced by co-founder Jerry Yang. This, in turn, boosted morale again, and I personally felt more optimistic about the company's outlook. Yahoo! was losing share in the global web audience, reaching 60 percent of monthly internet users,[12] compared with 70 percent when I had joined. If there was any possibility of turning this trend around, I felt that Yang was the person most likely to move the necessary mountains since Yahoo! was his baby, so to speak.

Yang performed a 100-day review and shared that Yahoo! would focus on "becoming a 'starting point' for the most consumers on the Web; extending its advertising offerings to sites across the Web; and opening up Yahoo's technology infrastructure to third-party developers and publishers."[13] This was a sound list, but one that wasn't aiming to reinvent the company so much as simplify its offerings and position it for cost-cutting. It also declared a vision of Yahoo's role in the web which employees could get behind. What wasn't obvious was that it would put Yahoo! in the middle of an intense showdown between the top two sites on the web.

Yahoo!'s desire to become a starting point for the most consumers on the web could only be achieved by getting ahead of its competition. Google now had the largest global audience on the web, followed by Microsoft and Yahoo!. Google and Microsoft achieved their top rankings quite differently, however. Google competed in an open playing field to create the highest-quality search engine on the market, whereas Microsoft took an indirect path that involved establishing a web-browser monopoly, for which it faced an antitrust lawsuit in 1998, and then setting the web browser's default starting point to msn.com, Microsoft's web portal.

Yahoo!'s strategy was unclear, but perhaps it didn't matter because the relevance of a web starting point was about to take a big hit. The month that Yang became CEO of Yahoo!, Apple released its first iPhone. The web browser on a desktop computer would soon be supplanted by a list of apps (applications) on a smartphone home screen, only one of which would be a web browser. Yahoo! had already developed non-web internet apps such as Yahoo! Instant Messenger, which was a free messaging desktop computer app, but the bulk of Yahoo!'s products were web-based. Likewise, "dot-com industry" would be supplanted with "tech industry," a broader domain that included mobile devices and their platform-specific applications. Becoming the most popular web starting point would have been an enormous achievement in the dot-com industry, but it was only a small slice of the pie in the tech industry.

In the context of the creation story of an online world, this was a huge moment of discovery and self-awareness—the web wasn't the center of the online universe. It was the equivalent of a single planet in the "tech" planetary system within an unknown galaxy. Perhaps the online universe didn't have the same hierarchy as the physical universe, but it was clear that the web was part of something much, much bigger.

Yahoo! also faced external challenges to extending its advertising offerings to sites across the web. It was a new area of competition with Google and Microsoft. In this case, Yahoo! had the lead market share in display ads on the web (a display ad is graphics-based rather than text-based). In April 2007, Yahoo! acquired an ad exchange, Right Media, to expand its display ad business across the web. An ad exchange is a plat-form where advertisers and publishers can respectively buy and sell advertising space via online auctions. At the same time, Google bought one called DoubleClick, outbidding Microsoft which shortly after snapped up another, AdECN. Google's purchase of DoubleClick was especially interesting since it hadn't previously been in the display ad business. The ads on Google were purely text-based, while Yahoo!'s and Microsoft's were a mix of graphics and text. The race was now on between the three web giants.

Next were the internal challenges Yahoo! faced after its

100-day review. There was the organizational fallout from deprioritizing and consolidating various Yahoo! sites. For example, Yahoo! stopped providing support to Yahoo! 360 Degrees (Yahoo!'s social networking site released in 2005) and shut down Yahoo! Photos (Yahoo!'s photo sharing site released in 2000) to focus on Flickr. Many employees began jumping ship to places that were growing, like Facebook. The cafeteria was filling up with displaced employees looking for new roles. It was a free-for-all. Employees had a unique chance to carve out impactful roles for themselves that would also benefit the company, provided they could find and convince the right decision-makers. However, they could also fall through the cracks amid the chaos.

During this time, a brilliant and ambitious engineering leader from Yahoo! Search took the initiative to consolidate data analysts across Yahoo! into a new team, product intelligence engineering (PIE), responsible for building a Hadoop data platform and analyzing the data. My team was part of this consolidation. I was told that the vision for PIE was to replace Yahoo!'s centralized data team, which was regarded as "too slow." I wasn't interested in upending another team, but there were rumors of layoffs and I was grateful to have a job that felt safe at that moment. Most of my original team found other roles in Yahoo! Media Group and we split up. Fortunately, my new boss was the teammate who trained me when I joined Yahoo!, which helped with the abrupt transition.

At the end of January 2008, Yahoo! officially announced it was planning to lay off approximately 1,000 of its 14,000 employees. Up to that point, apart from when CNET did layoffs during the 2000 dot-com crash, I hadn't been too worried about job security. These layoffs were different. Even if I kept my job, the future of the company was uncertain so my job would be uncertain too.

A couple of days later the uncertainty level skyrocketed. Microsoft announced an offer to buy Yahoo! for $44.6 billion. The combined global audience of Microsoft and Yahoo! was estimated to be 13 percent higher than Google's.[14] Yahoo!'s stock soared 48 percent on the news.[15] Google CEO Eric Schmidt openly objected to the potential deal: "We are concerned that there are things Microsoft could do that would be bad for the internet. We would hope that anything they did would be consistent with the openness of the internet, but I doubt it would be."[16] If a deal were reached, it would have an enormous impact on employees, consumers, shareholders, and the web. I personally didn't want to work for Microsoft or be laid off by them during the consolidation, so I hoped the deal wouldn't go through.

A week and a half later I turned on the local news and heard that Yahoo! had rejected Microsoft's offer, saying it was too low. My first reaction was, *I wonder what Jerry Yang's mother thinks*, assuming she was alive. I couldn't imagine chitchatting with my mother about the weather, what I ate for dinner, and an unsolicited $44.6 billion offer from a company found by U.S. courts and the European Commission to have abused its monopoly. When Yang became CEO, he asked Apple CEO Steve Jobs for guidance. I wondered who he turned to now for counsel other than his co-founder and the board. I imagined his mother would have a more interesting perspective to offer than anyone in the industry.

The following morning, the local news announced that Yahoo! would be doing layoffs that day (Yahoo! was on the local news frequently). I saw one of the purple Yahoo! mobiles in its usual spot when I got to work. When I left work it was gone, and I never saw it again. I wondered many times if a laid-off employee had to suffer the indignity of driving that car home. I was relieved to find out my job was safe, but witnessing the layoffs was highly uncomfortable. People were told in a conference room and then had to go back to their cubes to pack their belongings in front of their colleagues. Nobody knew if it was better to offer a hug or say nothing at all. I wouldn't have wanted to talk to anyone. Some people were let go due to performance issues and others because they were on the wrong project. It was like a giant game of musical chairs. There weren't enough jobs for everyone and one had to be lucky, skilled, and/or strategic to stay in the game.

In March and April, the discussions with Microsoft escalated. Unable to reach a deal, Microsoft CEO Steve Ballmer threatened a hostile takeover of Yahoo!. Yahoo! went on the defensive, seeking potential partnerships, including with Google. In one of the employee forums, someone joked that Yahoo! stood for You Always Have Other Options. Yahoo! had crossed paths with Google many times over the years and the twists and turns felt like a soap opera. I hoped Google or someone else would rescue us (and the web) from Microsoft's bullying.

Yang did a presentation to Microsoft, and the outcome was that Ballmer realized a hostile takeover wouldn't work. A person on the Microsoft team said, "They are going to burn the furniture if we go hostile. They are going to destroy the place."[17] Microsoft ended up walking away from the deal. Yahoo!'s shareholders were upset for being deprived of the money they would have made. I couldn't help but wonder what Yang had said in his presentation to elicit Microsoft's change of heart. I wish I had been a fly on the wall! He was a quiet person, but I could envision him fiercely protecting his creation. I was glad to work at Yahoo! while he was CEO.

In another twist, Google and Yahoo! began testing Google-generated ads in Yahoo! Search. Now it was Microsoft raising antitrust concerns. In response, Google co-founder Sergey Brin said, "We really believe in companies having choices about their destiny. Certainly a [Silicon] valley company like Yahoo—we want to support their ability to have choice. They were under hostile attack and we want to make sure they have as many options as possible."[18]

The balance of power on the web was at stake, but this particular situation hadn't evolved from healthy competition. It felt more like a forced game of tug-of-war initiated by Microsoft against Google. Microsoft tried paying Yahoo! to join their side to overpower Google, then they tried threatening Yahoo!, and now they were trying to disqualify Yahoo! and Google for teaming up to defend themselves against being strong-armed. My kindergarten class had played more maturely than this. Perhaps Microsoft needed to do more finger painting instead of finger pointing.

In May, negotiations with Microsoft re-opened on a smaller scale, to acquire only part of Yahoo!. In June, Yahoo! and Google officially announced their search ad partnership, and the Senate Antitrust Subcommittee immediately declared its plans to investigate the deal. Simultaneously, Yahoo!'s chief data officer and a number of other leaders departed ahead of a major Yahoo! reorganization. Some of my friends in the industry got in touch with me because they were seeing Yahoo! in the news more often, and not in a positive way.

With the mounting tension at all levels of the company and the industry, I began to feel nagging anxiety. I tried to explain it to a couple of people outside of the industry, but my concerns were dismissed and I was told to stop complaining about my cushy job. My best friend at the time wasn't able to find a graphic design job even though he was extremely talented and high-performing with the latest skills. Hiring criteria had become narrower, and being unconventional he just didn't fit the mold. The trouble was if he didn't find a job soon he would be homeless. He fell into a depression.

I instinctively turned to nature to feel more at peace. My best friend and I went on a hike and some people we met on the trail spoke enthusiastically about the Tule Elk Reserve at Point Reyes National Seashore (PRNS). When I googled it, I came across an upcoming volunteer tule elk docent program and immediately knew I needed to join. It took place on weekends during the elk rut (mating) season, so we would be pointing out behaviors like sparring, bugling, and harem formation to visitors.

The training was organized and led by one of the park rangers in the PRNS's Division of Interpretation & Resource Education. Several rangers and long-time volunteers with different areas of expertise taught us. We learned how to use multi-sensory, interactive tools and statistics to tell a story which helped visitors connect with the tule elk and the park. For example, we had visitors pass around a couple of tule elk antlers to get a feel for the weight and size, which were impressive. To my delight, we also used laminated slides including a tule elk population graph and an animal kingdom taxonomy hierarchy. Basically, this was a data insights job for environmental stewardship instead of profit. I loved the entire experience and barely noticed that the commute was nearly three hours each way from my apartment.

The interpretive techniques I learned at PRNS, especially the storytelling, would help me throughout the rest of my data career. A common challenge for data analysts is to drive change in their organizations, which can be difficult when they are lower down the pecking order than those they are trying to convince. Learning how to quickly assess a stakeholder's goals, values, and communication style helped me frame data insights to increase the chances of my work being used.

In August, my boss resigned and went to Google. I was sad to see him go. One day, a co-worker and I visited him for lunch at the Google cafeteria, which was known for its free gourmet food. It was my first time eating oysters on the half shell, and I licked my fingers. My co-worker and I then shamelessly stuffed our pockets with free chocolates, as though we had never seen food before. This was life at the headquarters of the top website in the world, just five miles from Yahoo!'s headquarters, where we were rationing office supplies.

My co-worker had driven us to Google in a Yahoo! employee shuttle van. As part of Yahoo!'s cost-cutting measures, some of the professional shuttle drivers had been let go and employees took turns driving the vans and parking them at their homes in return for personal-use privileges. My co-worker used the shuttle for weekend trips with his friends, and it was one of the reasons he chose to stay at Yahoo!. In contrast, Google lavished its employees with free dinners, onsite daycare, and onsite laundry, encouraging them to stay at the office longer. I preferred Yahoo!'s reduced perks because it resulted in a better work/life balance. Everyone at Yahoo! went home for dinner, which was one of the top reasons I chose to stay there.

In September, the leader of PIE resigned from Yahoo! to co-found the first Hadoop vendor, Cloudera, along with two engineers from Google and Facebook and an executive from Oracle. Hadoop was going strong in the industry, with Yahoo! having just used it to set a speed record for sorting one terabyte of data. Cloudera went on to release a commercial distribution of Hadoop and become an industry leader in enterprise data management. Meanwhile, the departure of PIE's leader and creator left the team in an awkward position.

On September 29, 2008, the stock market crashed. A few weeks later, Yahoo! announced it would be laying off 10 percent of its workforce.[19] It was unclear what PIE's fate would be since it was in organizational limbo and our team meeting was canceled every week. At one point we each had to do a slide presentation of our achievements in the past year to a set of leaders who were evaluating us. Our jobs were on the line. I began wearing interview clothes to work every day because we were under observation.

In November 2008, Google canceled its search ad partnership with Yahoo! after the Department of Justice said it would file an antitrust lawsuit to block it. A couple of weeks later, Yang announced that he would be stepping down as CEO but would remain in place until a new CEO was hired. It was unfortunate that much of his tenure was spent managing external drama instead of rebuilding the company from the inside out. I looked back at 2008, and it felt like riding an erratic roller-coaster on the verge of derailing. All I did was tightly grip the safety bar to avoid being thrown from the ride instead of holding on lightly and having fun. I couldn't relax and enjoy myself, and I realized it was time to look for a new job.

My job search was brief. First, I reminded myself that a few employees who left Yahoo! had returned saying, "It's even crazier out there than it is here!" Second, the job market was unfavorable due to the stock market crash. Lastly, data job descriptions had changed in such a way that I was turned off. They became narrower, inflexible, and purely technical. It sounded like the ideal candidates would be robots. This was consistent with what my best friend had experienced in his job search. I loved big-picture, open-ended projects that blended art and science. I didn't see any data job listings like this. I had caught a glimpse of the craziness out there. The good news was that it made me feel much better about my job at Yahoo!. I appreciated my projects and decided to focus on getting as much data experience as I could.

Two weeks before Christmas, I turned on the morning news and saw that Yahoo! would be doing the layoffs that day. Getting workplace updates on the news seemed to be the routine now, and I was grateful for the heads-up. If I was going to lose my job, I decided to go out in style, so I put on a nice dress and sparkly platform shoes. I kept almost nothing on my desk so I could just grab my backpack and walk out the door. To my relief, I was spared, as was most of PIE. Even though I had survived, I couldn't fully relax. At this point, layoffs were continuous. There was a legal requirement to announce larger rounds ahead of time, but individual employees were being let go without warning on a regular basis.

PIE was then moved under a marketing team. An engineering team in marketing? It seemed like a comical mismatch, but I had been wishing for marketing training to help with the ongoing presentations concerning the future of my job. I was also ready to try something new, though I had mixed feelings about marketing. My underlying concern was that by highlighting positives and omitting negatives, it could be quite misleading. Marketing is a wonderful tool if it is used to help consumers connect with products and services that benefit them. But what if it steers consumers toward harm? For many years, cigarette ads showed smiling, happy people smoking and having a great time, with no mention of the health hazards, until legislation was passed banning the ads. Yahoo!'s products and services didn't seem harmful to me, so I put my worries aside and went with the flow.

Unfortunately, the person in the marketing team who inherited PIE was another displaced employee who was not a marketer and didn't seem to know what to do with us.

Strategically, we were vulnerable in the game of musical chairs, so my boss started to look for a new home for the team.

In January 2009, Carol Bartz joined Yahoo! as the new CEO and Yang returned to his role as Chief Yahoo!. Bartz was a seasoned professional. Among her many achievements, she had been the CEO of Autodesk for fourteen years, quintupling its annual revenue during her tenure. More importantly, she was wise, experienced, well rounded, and decisive and brought a more feminine energy to Yahoo!. Her dynamic personality and colorful language resonated with employees, resulting in a lot of cheering and applause at her first all-hands (a corporate term for a leader's meeting with their entire organization). Yahoo! had a big problem with leaks to the press, and Bartz declared she would "drop-kick to fucking Mars"[20] any employees found doing so. People hoped the perpetrators would be caught just to see that! I was hopeful that Bartz would bring structure to Yahoo!'s nebulous organization so we would have a fighting chance to heal and move forward.

We all knew that another round of layoffs would probably be coming as part of the reorganization. My boss was getting closer to finding a new home for PIE and told us to keep it under our hats, which I did. One day, someone from the team met with him at 4 p.m. and made plans to continue their discussion the following morning, but our boss never showed up. The employee looked up his profile on the company's intranet and found that it had disappeared. We speculated that management discovered he was trying to move the team and let him go. Unfortunately, our boss hadn't saved his work on the team's annual reviews to the evaluation system, which meant that his reviews as well as our peer reviews were gone. My final review consisted of a few generic sentences prepared by someone who had met me twice in a group setting.

Basically, a year of work history was missing from my record, which made me feel angry and frustrated.

Right after our reviews, the person who did them also disappeared from the intranet, then his boss disappeared, and so on, until every person between PIE and Bartz was let go. PIE was temporarily placed under one of the chiefs of staff, who went extraordinarily above and beyond to find the proper home for us. Meanwhile, 5 percent of Yahoo!'s employees were laid off due to the recession's impact on online advertising (Yahoo!'s profit had dropped 78 percent year over year).[21] PIE was unaffected by the layoffs because the chief of staff advocated for us. We were given a free pass this time.

I found myself starting to wear makeup to work for the first time, perhaps because the chief of staff and CEO were female and I no longer had to be one of the guys. My cube was on the same floor as Bartz's office, and I saw her in the kitchen microwaving her lunch one day. Down to earth, she chatted with me while waiting for her food to heat. Things felt like they were looking up.

I had connected with someone from the B2B (business-to-business) marketing team in my row. He was analyzing display ad effectiveness, which was an area of the business I wanted to learn more about. I started working on bits and pieces of the project. Eventually, the B2B marketing team reorganized and PIE was moved there, along with some other employees. I was happy with the move, but some others wanted to remain in engineering and left the company.

In July 2009, Yahoo! and Microsoft announced a ten-year search partnership in which Microsoft's technology would power searches for both companies and Yahoo!'s salesforce would manage premium search advertiser sales for both companies. By this time, Google had 65 percent of the U.S.

search market share, Yahoo! had 20 percent, and Microsoft had 8 percent,[22] so combining forces wouldn't be enough to catch up with Google. The hope was that search profits would increase by pooling engineering resources and consolidating the buying process for advertisers. Yahoo!'s board supported the deal but shareholders were disappointed. Yahoo!'s stock price dropped 12 percent on the news and Microsoft's rose 1 percent.[23] Within a few weeks of the announcement, Doug Cutting left Yahoo! Search to join Cloudera and his Hadoop co-founder, Mike Cafarella, who was already there. This felt like a significant loss of talent to the Yahoo!-Microsoft search deal, which hadn't even got off the ground yet.

Fortunately, the deal didn't affect the display ad projects I was working on. Search ads were primarily text-based and "pulled" consumers looking for a particular product to an advertiser's website. For example, searching for "hotel" might bring up a text ad with a link to hotels.com to book a room. The ads on the rest of Yahoo! were primarily graphics-based and "pushed" an advertiser's product information to a target audience. For example, Domino's Pizza might use a display ad on Yahoo!'s homepage a few days before the Super Bowl to tell tens of millions of Americans about their game-day deal. These were the types of ads I would be focusing on.

Yahoo! had recently started selling new display ad formats that were pricier, such as video ads, and the sales team needed performance metrics to justify the higher cost. I was part of the team that worked on a series of projects to provide the information. This work felt highly impactful since Yahoo!'s display ad revenue had declined so dramatically. The ad effectiveness studies could help reverse the bleeding, save jobs, and sustain free content for users.

As we worked on the projects, we had a lot to learn from

my boss. He created stunning slides: each one had layers of information to uncover, like finding hidden meaning when gazing at a painting in a museum. He was even more gifted at building relationships. When he walked into a room, he seemed to know just about everyone and they were all delighted to see him. He arranged for the team to go "on tour" with our projects and get input from a wide variety of subject matter experts to ensure we had all angles covered and solid results. He connected us with someone in sales packaging to edit our final slides for external use, and by the end, I was certain they would help the sales team generate more revenue. My boss sincerely loved what he did, and he wanted everyone to leave a room more successful than when they entered it.

During the same period, we also had a lot to learn from my favorite data storyteller, who was in a different organization at Yahoo! but shared his work with my group. His latest study showed that Facebook was the biggest threat to Yahoo! at the time, even though they weren't a direct competitor. Web users only had so much time and, as more of them kept joining Facebook and ramping up their time there, they spent less time at their old favorites like Yahoo!. Somehow, he told this story with such humor and wit, focusing on the possibilities, that I was energized to find a creative way forward instead of feeling discouraged.

I treasured this time, which reminded me of the creative, collaborative culture in the earlier days of the web. I also knew that things changed quickly at Yahoo! and to enjoy this situation while it lasted.

I had the privilege of presenting the team's first ad effectiveness study at the B2B marketing all-hands. Several people I didn't know approached me afterwards with positive feedback. The biggest compliment I received was from someone in public relations who submitted my name as a candidate to be the keynote speaker at a conference. My boss and another person in my management chain told me how pleased they were with the talk and had me present a shorter version at a 400-person sales organization call.

A few weeks later, a friend in the audience sent me a message on Yahoo! Instant Messenger (YIM) to meet her for tea. When we met, she brought up the presentation and said that my boss had mentioned to her that he was very happy with it. She then said, "I can't understand why he made a big deal about it. It was just an average talk. Anyone could have done it." She didn't mention specifics on what she felt was lacking or offer any suggestions on how to improve it.

This was one of five negative encounters I had with co-workers that originated on YIM within a short space of time. A different woman messaged "You're useless" when I didn't know the answer to a question about her project but provided the name of someone who might be able to help. Another woman wrote "You're worthless" when I gave a detailed explanation of how to approach an analysis after she asked for my advice. Yet another woman asked me to send a link for a report someone else had created. She kept insisting the link I sent was incorrect, even though it was correct. She refused to click on it, saying that it looked longer than she remembered. I suggested that she ask the author of the report for the link, and she replied that she didn't want to bother him. Eventually, she told me in person that she hated all people of my ethnic background. The fifth negative encounter was with a male who was harassing me on YIM and in person. He criticized everything from my hairstyle to my shoes and effectively told me that as a woman I should know my place. I suppose the four women were sending a similar message. They all felt that I needed to stay small.

My head was swirling with questions. Why were 80

percent of these negative interactions with women when approximately 80 percent of my co-workers were men? And why was YIM the channel of choice for initiating this type of behavior? Why not email? Better yet, why not walk over to my cube and say these things out loud? Something about instant messaging was enabling, even though there was a transcript. It didn't make sense to me. I became stressed by these interactions and felt a twinge in the pit of my stomach every time I saw that I had a new message on YIM. Would it be from another "troll"?

I tried to keep the negativity in proportion by looking at it from a data perspective. I reminded myself that I started using instant messaging apps in 1988, when Internet Relay Chat (IRC) launched. My first twenty years of experience with instant messaging was neutral or positive, with the exception of one boss who was a micromanager. So, 99.9 percent of my interactions had been without incident, which was something to celebrate. Even though my five negative encounters led me to feel like "everyone" was demeaning, when I looked at the numbers I saw that they represented only a small percentage of my YIM contacts. I also heard that others had problems with the same people, which helped me realize that it wasn't personal. What's more, it helped me direct my energy toward people who were more constructive and collaborative.

I googled why women bullied other women at work and was struck by the number of theories. One suggested that society's expectations for female behavior conflict with criteria for success in the workplace, which is based on masculine attributes, and that women find it easier to release their frustration on other women instead of men. Another talked about how there were fewer opportunities for women in the workplace, so undermining the competition was one of the strategies for getting ahead. A third attributed it to narcissism. The truth was, there were no simple answers. The female bullies themselves probably couldn't pinpoint why they spent their energy bringing down other women using back channels like YIM.

The part that remained unsettling to me was how some of the bullies acted like model employees in group settings and then behaved badly behind the scenes. They were an unpredictable mix of affection and insults. Perhaps the looming threat of layoffs had put them in "frenemy" mode, acting like they were a friend one minute and an enemy the next. I had no idea how to deal with this type of behavior except to proceed with caution.

I missed my original team at Yahoo!. A few of us met for lunch one day, including my former boss at Google, and it was very comforting. I was with friends. I found myself unloading my challenges at work and in my personal life. Looking back, I should have been talking to a therapist, but I had no awareness of therapy at the time. My colleagues were kind, and their professional problem-solving skills came in handy. One suggested I join Facebook to perk up my social life. The co-worker who was a Yahoo! shuttle van driver suggested that I join the boot camp at the Yahoo! gym. It was the only other reason he stayed at the company, besides being able to drive the van for personal use. I had no idea what boot camp was, but I was willing to try anything.

Boot camp turned out to be a mix of cardio and strength exercises, most of which I had never done before and couldn't keep up with, but I had a fantastic time. It was pure play, and everyone was welcomed. The instructor tailored workouts for the campus, such as doing laps around it, running up and down the stairs of the parking garage, and jumping up and down on benches. There was no drama or weirdness, just a supportive and fun environment. It instantly became my top reason for working at Yahoo!.

My projects shifted at the same time as I started boot camp, and I enjoyed this new phase. I began providing quarterly commentary to the investor relations team about large upswings or downswings in Yahoo!'s sites. I also collaborated with a woman who was leading a study on Right Media ad exchange's high-level trends, for which I provided data insights. It was very pleasant working with her.

During this work, I got firsthand experience of "retargeting." Retargeted display ads are aimed at consumers who searched for a relevant term in the past or visited the advertiser's website but didn't make a purchase. The ad typically has an image of the item the consumer was browsing in the hopes they will click on it and pick up from where they left off. One day at work, I had a bra snafu and I searched for a replacement on my work laptop without thinking about it. Later, I was sharing my screen with a male co-worker for a project and while we were surfing Yahoo! a display ad popped up of a woman wearing the bra I had looked at. Why couldn't my first retargeted ad be for something less embarrassing like shoes or an airplane ticket! My face turned red. All my co-worker wanted to know was how he could get the same ad.

While I supported the advertising model on the web that kept many websites free, this type of targeting went too far for me. In the physical world, it would be like a salesperson from Macy's following me to the bank and popping up in front of me to ask if I wanted to come back and complete my bra purchase. If I hadn't been working on display ad insights, I would have started using an ad blocker. In our ad effectiveness studies, we found that some of the ad formats and placements had gone too far in disrupting the user experience, resulting in visitors leaving. For example, Yahoo! sometimes showed a thirty-second ad before a short video with no option to skip it after the first few seconds. This led to a high user-abandonment rate that was a lose-lose-lose for advertisers, users, and Yahoo!. To my surprise, retargeting ads performed well so they were here to stay. Finding the right balance of display advertising targeting, format, design, placement, and price continued to be a fascinating data puzzle for me.

During this time I also created a Facebook account. I was finally ready to see what all the hoopla was about, and I also wanted to try out Yahoo!'s new Facebook integration experience. Yahoo! was addressing Facebook's rising dominance on the web by working with it instead of against it, which seemed like a wise strategy. Web users could log in to many of Yahoo!'s sites with their Facebook accounts to share Yahoo! content on Facebook. They could also see their Facebook feed and update their Facebook status from Yahoo!'s homepage. The original intention of the web was to provide a seamless, interconnected experience, and the Facebook integration on Yahoo! felt true to that, a win-win for the websites and their users.

Facebook seemed like an amazing platform. I was able to reconnect with long-lost friends within minutes. But, then, it didn't take long to feel stressed out. As I went through my friends' profiles, I saw that some were consistent with who they were in real life and I enjoyed their updates, but others took on a completely different persona and I felt the same twinge in my stomach that I had with YIM. A couple of friends were completely obnoxious, reminding me of people who revealed their ugly side when they drank, and I wanted to "unfriend" them pronto. I was telling someone about my experience and they pointed out that "unfriend" was *New Oxford American Dictionary*'s word of the year in 2009.[24] That sounded like a good choice.

By this time, Facebook was no longer sorting the News Feed chronologically. It was using an algorithm named EdgeRank that predicted which content a user was most likely to engage with based on affinity (the past level of interaction with the poster), weight (weighted value of action types on the content, such as comments and likes), and decay (the age of the content). Users needed to choose who they engaged with wisely since EdgeRank mirrored their activity back to them, "amplifying" their choices.

The most eye-opening thing for me about Facebook was when I sat down to write a post of my own, I realized that I didn't have a single thing I wanted to say to all of my friends, acquaintances, co-workers, and family. The spectrum of relationships, communication styles, backgrounds, and values that made up my social circle was so broad I was at a loss for words. Facebook understood that not all "friends" are equal and provided options for creating different lists or sharing posts with only a subset of friends. As a data analyst, maybe I should have been excited to categorize my connections, but I didn't want to manage my social life like a marketing vendor's email lists nor my friendships to be transactional and engineered.

In the physical world, I tended to avoid large gatherings and preferred one-on-one or small group interactions. It felt natural to me to catch up with acquaintances only once or twice a year. I realized that Facebook did not suit that type of relationship dynamic and I became a "lurker," looking at other people's updates and rarely contributing to the conversation. I posted a few times to try it out but ended up using my account mainly for work research. I understood the appeal of Facebook and why many web users were dedicating so much time to it, but concluded it wasn't for me.

Yahoo! was experimenting with deepening its integration with Facebook and asked employees to participate. If we opted to give Yahoo! access to our Facebook accounts, we could see our Facebook updates on Yahoo!. In turn, our activity on Yahoo! would automatically be published on Facebook as part of the News Feed, in the hopes of engaging more Facebook users with Yahoo! content. I thought this went too far so I didn't opt in, but I did see articles in my News Feed from co-workers who did. One was a Yahoo! article about Taylor Swift in a bikini. When I clicked on it and saw the bikini picture, it reminded me of my bra retargeting ad and I laughed out loud. Maybe Yahoo! would regain its momentum if it showed enough bras and bikinis? It felt like some form of online littering. The "frictionless sharing" feature went live, but Facebook ended up discontinuing it. Like advertisers, users needed to strike a balance of what they were sharing and with whom and how often.

I felt like I needed a break from the online world. The web had surpassed a trillion unique URLs[25] vying for our attention. Users were being forced on the defensive, having to say "no" or "enough." I started to feel drained using the internet daily, even though I was paid to do so. The online world reminded me of being in a Las Vegas casino—I had no idea what time of day it was, I was surrounded by people unleashing repressed versions of themselves, I knew the experience was engineered to keep me there to maximize revenue, and I had to rely on self-control to walk away. At least for me trips to Las Vegas were few and far between and "what happens in Vegas stays in Vegas." In contrast, the online world was available continuously and what happened there followed people through time and space. The internet was no longer fun to me.

I began immersing myself in nature and regularly visited my best friend, who had found a job in the public sector and moved to the ocean. He was much happier than in Silicon Valley, and now I was the one in a depression. He encouraged me to move to the coast, but it would have quadrupled my commute so I was hesitant to do so. I kept visiting and felt the healing power of the beautiful, wild landscape. I noticed I was happiest when I was outdoors, away from the internet, like being on the trail at Point Reyes or doing jumping jacks on the lawn at boot camp.

I decided to go on vacation in nature and felt refreshed when I got back. While I was away, my boss had resigned. The head of Yahoo! AdLabs generously volunteered to lead the team while helping to find a replacement for my boss. He took the time to get to know us and ask each of us what we wanted to do next. He prioritized our well-being, which in my experience was rare among senior leadership. We were very lucky to have him in our court.

Earlier in the year, Carol Bartz had hired a new chief product officer, who would lead Yahoo's consumer and advertising products, including display ads. Our team had been slated to move there, and we officially did around the time of my boss's departure. The product team didn't have any space available for us, so, without any notice, the marketing organization exiled us to a remote building away from our stakeholders. We stayed there while the cubes sat empty in the marketing area. Within days another round of layoffs was announced, rumored to affect the product organization. I was still feeling at peace from my vacation and knew I would be fine no matter what happened. I was getting much better at handling layoffs.

The head of Yahoo! AdLabs helped us move from the product organization to the data organization. Whether it was to protect us from layoffs or simply a better fit, it seemed like a good idea to spend time in the data organization after years of working in satellite data teams in the media, engineering, marketing, and product organizations. Our new manager also came from the product organization, and we would be providing product insights. As part of the organizational change, we moved back to the main campus and we were back on track again, unaffected by the loss of 600 jobs.

While this was all good news, ever since my vacation I had a lingering sense of detachment from my job. I hadn't brought my cellphone with me on the trip and felt much happier without it. I realized that I needed to slow down and spend less time online because I was starting to feel overwhelmed by the pace and direction of change on the internet. I knew I needed to prioritize time in nature and that my physical and online worlds needed to be more in sync. I could see that data would play a huge role in keeping balance in the online world because it measured the impact of change, revealing when decision-makers had gone too far. That felt like important work, and I wanted to keep going as long as I didn't lose myself in the process.

I could see how much I had grown in the past few years. The sink-or-swim circumstances helped me become more resilient and confident. The more teams I worked for, the more I learnt and gained new perspectives. Even though this was all a byproduct of dysfunctionality instead of employee development, it was invaluable nonetheless. My sense of faith and trust in navigating the over-engineered, volatile environment began to develop.

One night I was sitting in my living room and, suddenly, I knew I was ready to move to the ocean. I pictured the kind of apartment I wanted, and then I called my best friend to let him know. He found an apartment on Craigslist that fit the description in the block next to him. He called the number and got us an appointment to see the place the next day. I fell in love with it immediately, and the landlord said we were the first ones who called so it was mine if I wanted it. I had forgotten the power of intuition and noticed that it had been subtly guiding me through the turbulence at work to spend more time in nature and the outdoors. It was coming through loud and clear now, perhaps because I was so relaxed after my vacation. I knew that the long commute would probably cause me to leave Yahoo! at some point. I decided that in whatever time I had left at the company, I would let my intuition steer the way and see what happened.

CHAPTER 2
AWAKENING

Many of the issues in Silicon Valley can be explained by its geography. The San Francisco Peninsula is approximately twenty miles wide by fifty miles long and is divided by the Santa Cruz Mountains, formed by the San Andreas Fault. To the east side of the Santa Cruz Mountains is Silicon Valley. It is a highly-developed industrialized area that is home to many of the top tech companies, including Apple, Google, and Facebook. To the west of the Santa Cruz Mountains is a natural wonderland of redwood forests and beaches lining the Pacific Ocean, with narrow, windy roads and spotty cell service.

This contrast has similarities to the Chinese philosophical concept of yin and yang: "The two great opposite but complementary forces at work in the cosmos. Yin is the female, cold, dark, passive power, yang represents masculinity, light, and warmth. Their balance is essential to harmony and health."[1] The redwood forests' feminine yin energy and Silicon Valley's masculine yang energy each have many positive attributes. The problem is that few roads traverse the Santa Cruz Mountains, so the two sides have remained somewhat isolated from each other, creating an imbalance. In Silicon Valley, aggressive growth has overwhelmed the infrastructure, creating crushing traffic, the most expensive housing marketing in the United States, and extreme competition for personal survival. On the west side, a "locals only" attitude has developed, with a fixation on the past.

It was my hope to feel more balanced by living next to the ocean while working in Silicon Valley. Indeed, my this was the case immediately, despite the longer commute. After work, I routinely met with my best friend and his neighbors in an English garden one of them had created. On weekends I explored the nearby redwood forests and tide pools, discovering a number of hidden gems. Nearby was a community thrift store that served as a central meeting place to catch up on news while connecting with unique items, such as a hand-carved wooden snake I scored and named Milo. People often sought counsel from the store owner when they had problems, and I began doing this myself. I also started meeting other residents by posting pictures of local scenery on Instagram, which was a relatively new app. I felt a sense of community for the first time since working in Silicon Valley.

Not everyone was welcoming, however. I definitely got a few "I hate tech people" and "Go back to where you came from" comments. Tech workers hadn't overtaken the area yet and locals feared the possibility of being priced out like the communities "over the hill," which is how those on the coast referred to the east side of the Santa Cruz Mountains. It didn't help that, in 2008, a tech billionaire purchased private property along a popular surfing beach in the area and closed it to the public, resulting in years of lawsuits to have access restored.

Living in nature felt exhilarating, but it also came with challenges. A couple of months after moving to the coast, my best friend called me in the middle of the night to let me know we had a tsunami warning. There had been a magnitude-9.1 earthquake in Japan followed by a tsunami that was expected to arrive at the California coast later that morning. The travel time from Japan to California was less than eleven hours, comparable to a non-stop flight from Tokyo to Los Angeles.

He told me not to panic and to wait and see what the impact would be in Hawaii. This would give us plenty of time to walk up the hill to safety if needed. Fortunately, we didn't need to escape. The tsunami arrived at low tide and stayed low. In Japan, nearly 20,000 people died and damages exceeded $200 billion, making it the most expensive natural disaster in history. In California, a number of harbors and docks sustained damages totaling $100 million. My area was unharmed, but we could see the change in the ocean's dynamics from something that happened more than 5,000 miles away.

Later, I read that during the Great East Japan Earthquake, as it was named, neighborhoods built on land that was reclaimed from the sea experienced "liquefaction," the shaking of soil saturated with water that turns it to liquid, and that liquefaction had also occurred in San Francisco's Marina District during the 1989 Loma Prieta earthquake.[2] Given that Yahoo!'s headquarters was located on the San Francisco Bay, I wondered if it was in an area prone to liquefaction. I learned that it was, and wished I hadn't found out. I doubted that my tiny, thin desk would offer much protection if the building sank and/or collapsed. I joked to myself that Yahoo! was on shaky ground both literally and figuratively.

I decided to go on a hike recommended by my best friend: to the epicenter of the Loma Prieta earthquake, which was a few miles west of the San Andreas Fault in a redwood forest. When I arrived at the epicenter, I saw a number of redwood trees strewn like toothpicks and some sections of earth that had slid a few feet. More than two decades had passed since the earthquake, but the epicenter was still in disarray. Twenty years barely registers in the timeline of California's coastal redwood forests, which are about 20 million years old, with trees that can reach 2,000 years of age. Loma Prieta's trees are relatively young because the area was clear-cut between 1883 and 1923. Even so, I felt a sense of timelessness standing in the epicenter, which contrasted sharply with the frenetic pace of the web. It seemed hard to believe that the web was conceived in the same year as the Loma Prieta earthquake. I thought about how Yahoo!'s offices were less than twenty-five miles away as the crow flies and built only a decade earlier, next to a sewage treatment plant. I had a hard time reconciling the two antithetical worlds.

My best friend, who had grown up in Berkeley in the 1960s, assigned me some reading, including Ram Dass's *Be Here Now*, published in 1971. Dass, whose birth name was Richard Alpert, was a psychology professor at Harvard University in the late 1950s and early 1960s. He and fellow Harvard lecturer Timothy Leary performed research experiments on the effects of psychedelic drugs on human consciousness (the drugs were legal at the time) until they were fired in 1963. In 1967, Alpert traveled to India and eventually found the guru he went on to study with. He returned to the United States as Ram Dass and wrote *Be Here Now* to share his spiritual journey and learnings. The book sold two million copies and was considered a "countercultural bible."[3]

After finishing the book, I began practicing meditation. At first I felt like nothing was happening, but over time I realized that my anxiety had decreased. I also bought myself a few decks of oracle cards to experiment with, since they reminded me of the imagery within the book: single-page illustrations that worked not only as standalone pieces but also related to each other as part of a series. The decks came with instruction booklets on how to do readings to provide "clarity and confidence" about a particular question or situation. I couldn't help but notice the similarities to my work on corporate data insights.

I used oracle card decks as a tool for developing my intuition, accessing my inner data, and applying the insights to my life. One of the first decks I purchased was nature-themed, which helped me realize that I had lost the sense of cycles and seasons in my life. In Silicon Valley, the weather is similar year-round and the tech industry has a culture of working continuously. There is no ebb and flow. In fact, in the online world there is no sunrise or sunset. It is always "on." I recalled that in 1998, when Yahoo! Games launched, I pulled an all-nighter playing bridge with strangers and rejoiced at the idea of being able to play cards all the time. The next day, when the lack of sleep caught up with me, I felt differently and never pulled an all-nighter again. Now that I was living at the coast, it would be easier to reconnect with nature's cycles. I made sure to stay aware of the moon phases and tides as well as the migration periods of whales and birds. I watched sunsets as though I had never seen them before. My perception of time shifted, and I felt more in tune with life and like a "normal" person again.

I wondered how these changes in my personal life would affect my data insights projects at Yahoo!. I soon had a new worthwhile project to use as my litmus test. Yahoo! started to sell a display ad format that took over an entire page for a few seconds, delaying users from accessing the page's content. Several of us in my cubes row groaned out loud when we first encountered it. I thought my web browser had frozen, so I closed it. My manager spoke with some decision-makers who thought this type of ad might drive users away. They wanted to quantify the impact on user experience. My boss asked me if I would be able to lead a study, and I leapt at the opportunity.

I was given the freedom to pick who I collaborated with and how to perform the study. Planning consisted of meditating, doing oracle card readings, and playing for a couple of days, which ended up saving efforts and resources overall. We were able to quantify the tradeoff between the increase in short-term revenue of the new ad format versus the decrease in long-term user retention. The results were used to strike a balance between these two critical metrics, and a frequency cap for the new ad format was negotiated between the stakeholders involved. The team who owned the new ad format expressed their unhappiness with the outcome. The challenge with striking a balance is that, often, some people have to give something up for the benefit of the whole without being rewarded for it.

I shared the study with the head of Yahoo! AdLabs and my favorite storyteller, both of whom gave positive feedback and encouraged more studies like it. I also presented the study at the data services all-hands and it was well received, with only one negative comment: a woman told me that the study wasn't much of anything. Overall, the experience was validating and I finally felt like I had found my stride. It was rewarding to use data to bring more balance to Yahoo!, and I hoped to continue. Unfortunately, I wasn't able to as the company was faced with more urgent issues.

Yahoo! had a sales reorganization that resulted in unexpectedly high turnover, which, in turn, had a negative impact on display ad revenue. Some of the sales staff resigned jointly and headed for trendier companies, such as Groupon. To make matters worse, Facebook was about to dethrone Yahoo! as the top display ad seller in the United States and Google was steadily gaining ground. Furthermore, Yahoo! was struggling with search ad revenue. Despite the alliance between Yahoo! and Microsoft, Yahoo!'s net search ad revenue was declining. Yahoo! couldn't afford to turn away any short-term ad revenue at this point, and balance now became a low priority.

Morale was declining again, and I noticed that some international employees were deciding to move back home because of the toxic work environment, high cost of living, and/or hesitancy to raise their children in Silicon Valley. One of my co-workers simply said, "This isn't worth it." I could relate. I had moved to the coast for similar reasons.

My team was reorganized and my boss moved to a different department. I stayed in the data organization, but my role shifted to responding to a variety of requests coming from my management chain. I started to see what was under the hood in the data organization, and it was mixed. Some parts worked well, such as the self-service tools and the data engineering team which supported several of the insights studies I had worked on. However, other things held Yahoo! back, such as a delay of years in the release of a new, more detailed internal reporting system and a lack of documentation on the wide variety of available data sources. I finally understood why the various satellite data teams across the company had been created as well as PIE's frustration with the data organization being "too slow."

Around this time, I noticed that the quality of the content I was being served on Yahoo!'s homepage was dropping substantially. In 2008, Yahoo! started using the Content Optimization Knowledge Engine (COKE) algorithm to decide the placement and duration of stories on Yahoo!'s homepage. Editors chose the pool of stories, and COKE continuously tested the click rates of these stories on small samples of users to determine the optimal combination to serve to other users. Editors monitored the results and learned from the feedback.

This seemed like a thoughtful use of technology to improve the human editorial process. However, a more personalized version of COKE had recently been released: Content Optimization and Relevance Engine (CORE) optimized content within age and gender groups. What ended up happening, in my experience, was a gender divide.

CORE was serving one of my male co-workers more sports stories while I was being inundated with celebrity gossip and fashion slideshows. The only sports stories I was served were about athletes' love lives or what they wore on the red carpet. The algorithm was simply reflecting the choices of each demographic group, and I was disappointed that women between the ages of thirty-five to forty-four so strongly favored stereotypical content.

As the quality of content reduced, the quantity increased. CORE was serving me celebrity slideshows around fifty images long daily, and I felt compelled to click all the way through to the end. I experienced a heaviness in my stomach when clicking through, like I had eaten too much junk food. It was like being served super-sized, deep-fried Twinkies for my brain. Instead, I wanted a balanced, thoughtfully-portioned bento box of content, with an occasional deep-fried Twinkie as a splurge. If I hadn't been an employee, I would have stopped using the site.

One weekend I was chatting with one of the other elk docents at Point Reyes. She asked where I worked, and when I told her she looked anguished. "The stories on Yahoo! have become so ... *trashy*," she said. "I feel like I'm reading a tabloid. Can't they *do* something about it?" Yes, it was definitely an option to set up the algorithm differently, but it would likely result in fewer clicks, which would equate to lower revenue, so it was highly doubtful. The CORE team was working on adding more variables to the algorithm, and I hoped it would result in a better experience.

One Tuesday I was working at my desk when, out of the blue, I received an email from Carol Bartz with the subject "Goodbye." She'd just been fired over the phone by Yahoo!'s chairman of the board. Employees found out later that she'd been on her way to New York at the time to host a Q&A at a conference the next day. Yahoo! was going through immense challenges, but the board could have handled Bartz's removal more smoothly and professionally. The board didn't comment on the reason for firing her so abruptly, but she certainly had something to say about it afterwards: "These people fucked me over."[4] It was announced that Yahoo!'s chief financial officer, Tim Morse, would be the interim CEO.

I was briefly shocked, then angry at the unnecessary drama, then anxious that the company would have to start all over again, and then at ease knowing things would probably turn out okay. I went through my grieving process in record time. I silently thanked Carol Bartz for the sense of hope and belonging she had given me and wished for her a much better setting than Yahoo!.

During the time between CEOs, I decided to catch up on doctor's appointments. I had my first routine mammogram after turning forty, and it came back abnormal. I went for a biopsy and was told I had early stage cancer and needed surgery. The doctor estimated a 30 percent chance that I would need chemotherapy after the surgery.

Until that point I hadn't had any major health issues, and I was unfamiliar with the healthcare system. I had no idea of what to expect or what questions to ask. I tried googling for more information and ran into personal tales of surgeries gone wrong. I couldn't bring myself to research chemotherapy. A couple of people recommended that I not tell anyone at work because I would likely be treated differently, and not in a good way. I checked in with my intuition, which was hard to hear with my fear screaming in the foreground, and it agreed that it would be better for me to not let people know about my situation unless I needed chemotherapy. I felt immediate relief. I wouldn't be drained by unsolicited advice and people projecting their fears and judgments onto me.

My best friend went above and beyond to support me. He created a magnificent wallscape of photographs he had taken of my favorite local tide-pooling spots, which he and his girlfriend installed in my living room. He also cooked a feast of my favorite foods and listened to my frustrations regarding the lack of information from my doctors. Even though he gave me peace of mind, I was still fearful of the unknown.

I looked at my life. I worked in a toxic place with stressed-out people. I was scared that cancer could lead to the loss of my job and rejection from other employers in the Valley. I disliked the direction the internet had taken and felt discouraged by my career outlook. I was still traumatized by the male co-worker bullying me on YIM. He had a habit of approaching me in the cafeteria and gym, coming within a few inches of me, hovering for a couple of seconds, and then walking away without saying a word. It was very creepy. I knew my life had many positive aspects, but at the time, the negative ones were dominating.

A couple of weeks before my surgery, I was feeling especially distraught and went to the redwoods. I hiked for a bit and stopped, overcome by emotion. I felt lost. Suddenly, an incredible surge of energy from the trees traveled through my body—it was almost electrical: a deep and instantaneous sense of knowing that I was going to be okay and I wasn't alone. I would be fine. I was loved. This energy from the trees engulfed me entirely. I felt a sense of weightlessness, and time was briefly suspended. I didn't know if the experience lasted a fraction of a second or a minute.

While I had spent a lot of time in nature, I had no background in spirituality or the supernatural. I also didn't do drugs. So, frankly, I was shocked by what had happened and had no explanation. I stood there and let it sink in. Then, a wave of euphoria came over me. The trees had talked to me, and it felt like a miracle! I walked around in a daze for a few days, feeling like I was deeply in love. It was indescribable.

When the feeling started to fade, it occurred to me that maybe if I went back to the redwoods it would happen again. I returned the following weekend and had a similar kind of experience.

When it was time for my surgery, I went into the hospital feeling optimistic. My best friend came with me, held my hand as I underwent general anesthesia, and celebrated with me when the results came back saying the margins were clear and I wouldn't need chemo.

At work, I told my boss about the surgery since I needed time off and approval to work from home while I recovered. He was completely supportive. The rest of the team knew I had permission to work from home, but not the specific reason. I was bullied on YIM by two female co-workers for working from home. Who did I think I was? Two male co-workers YIMed me to see if I was okay, and I felt comfortable telling them what happened. One of them recommended that I watch the documentary *Forks Over Knives*, which demonstrates the benefits of whole-food, plant-based diets in preventing and combating cancer. For me, it reinforced the idea of opting for less processing in whatever I consumed—whether it was food or content.

Somehow I felt less worried about the cancer returning than I did about the unknown effects of spending hours a day online for years at my job. I wondered if excessive consumption of toxic web content would lead to long-term mental health issues such as dementia. The guidance for preventing dementia includes healthy eating, routine exercise, and staying mentally and socially engaged. I was pretty sure that celebrity gossip and Facebook didn't qualify. Was I in a "hazardous" career? Being part of the first generation of web employees meant we were guinea pigs of sorts. I knew going forward I needed to prioritize taking care of myself, both physically and mentally.

In January 2012, Scott Thompson, who had been an executive at PayPal, became Yahoo!'s CEO. Two weeks later Jerry Yang abruptly left Yahoo!, including his position on the board of directors. There were no farewell celebrations, speeches, or emails from him. Thompson casually announced the departure as though just another employee had left. It felt extremely weird to me.

In February, the chairman of Yahoo!'s board of directors announced that four more people would be leaving the board, including himself. They named two new board members and said they would be searching for the other replacements. One week later, a hedge fund, Third Point, filed regulatory documents proposing four new board members, including Third Point's CEO, Daniel Loeb. Third Point owned nearly 6 percent of Yahoo! and was initiating a proxy fight.[5] Ironically, it was Valentine's Day and Loeb had sent similar letters on past Valentine's Days to three other businesses.

In March, Yahoo!'s board announced the three new board members who they felt were "more qualified for the position" than those proposed by Third Point.[6]

In April, Thompson carried out the largest layoffs in Yahoo!'s history: 14 percent of employees lost their jobs.[7]

In May, Third Point sent a letter to Yahoo!'s board about an inaccuracy they discovered in Thompson's résumé. He claimed to have degrees in accounting and computer science, when he had only an accounting degree. Less than two weeks later, Thompson decided to leave Yahoo! due to the issue with his résumé as well as a diagnosis of thyroid cancer. I found it interesting that Yahoo!'s board didn't call him over the phone to fire him as they did with Carol Bartz. Yahoo! executive Ross Levinsohn was named interim CEO, and Yahoo! ended the proxy fight with Loeb. Three of the four board candidates that Third Point had proposed on Valentine's Day joined Yahoo!'s board, including Loeb.

While I had become hardened to corporate carnage, the latest developments at Yahoo! reached new levels of drama and destruction. Everyone was disposable, from the board to the worker bees to the founders. Eight of the eleven members of the board of directors had been on the job for three months or less. The other three had been on the job for less than two-and-a-half years. And, despite being a global company, the board was all-white and had just one female. During my employment, there had been four CEOs, two interim CEOs, six rounds of layoffs, a hostile takeover attempt, and a proxy fight. I had worked for more than a dozen bosses; one of them had lasted for just a few hours. Yahoo! was a dying company, and it felt like a frenzy of greedy scavengers had descended upon it to squeeze out as much money as possible before its last breath.

What surprised me most was that almost nobody at work talked about the chaos. It made me feel like I was crazy. I went to the anonymous company review site, glassdoor.com, expecting to see low ratings in the recent reviews. Instead, the ratings were fairly high. Some employees had even rated their current experience at Yahoo! five out of five stars. I wondered what was going on. Then I read the reviews and understood. The reviewers were predominantly interns who were unaffected by the drama and treated very well in the hopes of converting them to full-time employees after graduation. New college graduates were the most coveted employees in Silicon Valley; their technical skills were cutting edge, their salaries were the lowest, and, perhaps most importantly, due to their lack of experience they tended to follow orders and not question management.

It also occurred to me that Yahoo! had a significant number of international employees in the U.S. offices. Some of these employees were on H-1B work visas and couldn't afford to rock the boat by expressing negative opinions or advocating for better conditions because they depended on Yahoo! for sponsorship. If they were fired and didn't have another job lined up, they could be deported. Their work visas weren't transferable to new employers, making it more difficult to switch jobs. This had been called out as modern-day indentured servitude, and I wondered if it was a calculated strategy to prevent tech employees from organizing and advocating for themselves.

A few years later, computer science professor Norman Matloff testified about the H-1B program to the U.S. House Judiciary Committee Subcommittee on Immigration. He presented four ways that corporations used the H-1B program to subsidize their labor costs. The one that benefited technology companies most, according to Matloff, was hiring younger H-1Bs over older Americans. Unfortunately, at forty-one years old I was considered "older" in the tech industry. In my job search after the Scott Thompson debacle, I was consistently being told that I was overqualified and that someone more junior would be a better fit. According to the federal government, I still had twenty-six more years until retirement. It didn't seem like I would be able to make it to the finish line with a career in tech.

I found it interesting that interviewers stopped asking

the classic question "Where do you see yourself five years from now?" A five-year horizon had become an obsolete concept. When I received my Yahoo! five-year anniversary gift of a gumball machine, the gumballs were stale. Yahoo! management had likely been overly optimistic in their estimation of employees who would stay for five years. Times had changed. Employers now wanted to know what you could produce for them when you walked through the door, and they hoped you would be gone long before five years were up.

I was stressed out by my lack of career prospects. I started spending as much of my free time as possible hiking in the redwoods, which helped tremendously. I didn't have any more "energetic experiences," but those two experiences before my surgery had helped deepen my connection.

I thought about how the trees had infused me with their resilience to help me through my surgery. I wanted to offer something in return and wondered what I could possibly give. Redwood trees are masters of time but not of space. That is to say, they can live for 2,000 years but are bound to a single location for their entire lives. On the other hand, I had been alive for a mere forty-one years but had traveled around the planet. So, I thought I could describe the outside world to them.

I went back to the area in the redwood forest where I'd had my energetic experiences. Drawn to a particular tree—its charred bark evidence that it had been through a fire—I walked up to it and put my palms on its trunk to see if I could feel its aliveness. I tried to synchronize my breathing with the tree and concentrated on attuning to its frequency. After a couple of minutes, a sensation traveled through my palms, then arms, then lower core: a gentle buzzing, a mellow energy. I felt like I had made a connection "into" the tree. (Later, I realized that the process reminded me of Spock's Vulcan mind meld on *Star Trek,* in which he would touch someone or some-thing and share thoughts.)

I tried to communicate with the tree using my mind to project images of places and things around the planet that I wanted to show it. Then I described the images out loud. I started with the Pacific Ocean, explaining that the fog from the ocean was a source of moisture for the tree. I described what the ocean looked like and its incomprehensible enor-mity. I held an image in my mind of a tremendous roaring wave crashing on the shore, demonstrating its dynamism and fluidity. I showed the tree gray whales migrating to Alaska, towering spires in the Utah desert, and the snow-capped Sierra Nevada mountains. Then I shifted toward human development and images of New York City with its bright lights and crowded subways, an NBA basketball game, an airplane soaring in the clouds, a Picasso painting, a casino in Las Vegas, cars on a highway, shopping malls, and the iPhone. I shared landscapes of countries across the planet and the wide variety of foods people ate. I showed other types of trees and explained that redwoods were the tallest trees in the world.

I regularly returned to the tree and had exchanges during which it would give me guidance and in return I would offer insights that might be complementary to its experience. This two-way exchange deepened my relationship with the tree and helped me get to know myself better. Sometimes I would just drop by to say hi, and other times it would be for deeper inter-actions. It felt like an intimate friendship.

When I asked the tree for guidance about my workplace, the suggestion came through to read about the "Immortal Tree." A roadside attraction on the Avenue of the Giants in northern California, the Immortal Tree is a living example of the redwood tree's resilience to trauma. I had visited a few times before but hadn't recognized its role as a teacher until my own redwood tree brought it to my attention.

The Immortal Tree is nearly 1,000 years old and has survived forest fires, a lightning strike that reduced its height by forty-five feet, a logging attempt in 1908 that left visible scars, and a flood in 1964 that submerged it under ten feet of water. How was it possible for the Immortal Tree to survive all these damaging events? When it comes to fight or flight, redwood trees have no choice but to fight. Their survival tools include an extremely thick protective bark that's fire- and insect-resistant, plus a wide, shallow root system for anchoring itself and extracting nutrients.

Applying this to my work situation, I thought that if I developed a thicker skin and connected at a deep level with people around me, I would have the capacity and support to endure whatever work (or life) threw at me. I also took it as a message that it was normal to encounter a variety of issues in one's lifetime and that the drama at Yahoo! was just one of many hurdles to overcome. I had the epiphany that I should seek out and connect with wise, mature, and resilient people. The first person who popped into my head was the owner of the thrift store, because so many people sought her out for advice. I found out later she had overcome many hurdles in her life and was basically a human version of the Immortal Tree. The tech industry's obsession with youth suddenly felt inconsequential. In "redwood time," I was just getting started! I hoped that someday I would be a wizened badass with cool scars marking the challenges I endured. That resonated in my core.

The next time I visited my redwood tree, I thanked it for steering me to the Immortal Tree for guidance and suddenly had the idea to play music for it. Since survival was a theme in our interactions, I started with the 1978 disco classic "I Will

Survive," explaining that humans often had to endure destructive behavior from other humans, both physical and emotional, similar to how the Immortal Tree had to endure logging from humans. Next, I played the 1979 new wave hit "Cars" by Gary Numan that captures the isolation people experience due to technology. As I stood with the tree, I recalled reading that Numan had symptoms of Asperger's syndrome, which can cause someone to have deep interests and talent but an inability to listen to others, interpret social cues, or express empathy.

I first heard about Asperger's about a decade earlier. It resonated since the symptoms described a lot of people I knew from work or school. In fact, one of the articles included someone I had gone to math camp with during high school. He ended up ostracized by some camp attendees and instructors due to his lack of social skills, which was saying a lot coming from a group of nerds. After reading the article, I felt terrible that I had avoided him at camp. I had assumed his off-putting behavior was intentional when it was actually a developmental disorder. I suddenly appreciated his communication style, which was like a programming language: logical, literal, concise, and free of adjectives, emotions, and filler words. He sounded abrasive at the time, but now I recognized that he was also sincere and trustworthy.

In 2013, Asperger's syndrome became part of autism spectrum disorder (ASD). I wondered how much of technology's effect of isolating people from each other was a reflection of the social isolation of its creators, whether due to ASD or other circumstances.

In other visits with the tree, I explored science versus spirituality. I had been trained in science for many years, but it couldn't explain certain things in my life. For instance, what were the energetic experiences I had with the trees before my surgery? And how did I "know" the precise moment to call my best friend about moving to the coast such that I landed the perfect apartment a block away from him?

The general answer I received was that these events were simply part of life. I interpreted that to mean that nature operates by what humans refer to as intuition or instinct. I didn't receive an answer from the tree on how intuition works, just that it is.

When I was among nature, it felt effortless to follow my intuition, but I wasn't sure if intuition would "work" in a toxic corporate environment. What if it steered me away from the toxicity into joblessness and homelessness? Did intuition factor into the human construct of money? Some online articles I'd read suggested that to gain confidence using intuition in big areas of life, it was helpful to start with small, low-risk decisions such as picking a brand of tea at the supermarket. This felt like a safe, scientific approach to ramping up, and I embraced it.

I started shopping at the supermarket by feeling drawn to certain items, the same way I was drawn to my redwood tree. One day, I bought rainbow chard and ended up using it to create a delicious soup. I was quite impressed with myself since I'd never purchased rainbow chard before, nor did I particularly enjoy cooking. I also found it reassuring that my intuition didn't lead me to fill my cart with junk food.

I applied the same concept at work by intuitively picking content to consume on Yahoo!. I found I was prioritizing quality over quantity. However, it was difficult to sustain. As soon as I lapsed into passivity, I would again find myself deep in a fashion slideshow quagmire with heaviness in my stomach.

The real test for using my intuition at work was about to come. In July 2012, Marissa Mayer became CEO of Yahoo! and joined its board of directors. She was a former Google executive who had started there in 1999 as Employee #20. During her tenure, she'd led the evolution of several major Google products, starting with Google Search, and worked her way up the ranks. She had a reputation for being incredibly intelligent, hands-on, and detail-oriented. Analysts and employees were extremely excited about her appointment, and there was optimism that she would be able to turn Yahoo! around the way Steve Jobs had turned Apple around.

Mayer didn't waste any time. The first weekend, she worked with the staff to transform the cafeteria. On Monday morning, employees were surprised to find that the menu was now free and full of high-end choices, similar to the cafeteria at Google. I remember many of us running around the dining area thrilled! This was the first CEO to spend money on employees instead of cutting costs and jobs.

Mayer was also the first CEO to give employees a collective voice by holding a company-wide all-hands every week. In advance of the all-hands, a site was set up for employees to submit and vote for questions. The executive staff was accountable for answering and following up on the top questions. I hadn't experienced anything like this in my career. The only hitch was that the questions couldn't be submitted anonymously, so they tended to be "safe" and non-controversial.

One of the early questions was if Yahoo! could provide onsite day care, which was a perk available at Google. The executive staff said they were open to it, but after research they learned that toxicity levels of the soil on campus were too high, in part due to past weapons testing at the location. I immediately wondered if the toxicity had played a role in the development of my breast cancer since exposure to toxic waste was known to cause cancer as well as shorten lifespan and create developmental disabilities in children. Interestingly, the employees around me seemed more disappointed that Yahoo! wouldn't have day care than they were about finding out their workplace was physically toxic.

Mayer also addressed the problem of leaks to the press, but her approach was different from that of Carol Bartz. One of the leaks after she joined had caused Yahoo!'s stock price to drop that day. She computed the value of the loss and said she'd sue the perpetrator for that amount if they were caught. I thought that was ingenious. After that announcement, there were a lot fewer leaks.

Mayer lived up to her reputation of being hands-on and detail-oriented. She personally reviewed the hiring process from start to finish, including evaluating résumés and reviewing the job offers extended. She suggested that Yahoo! needed more new college grads. To quickly ramp up, she planned to acquire companies which could fill the talent gaps she had identified, especially the lack of mobile engineers. Wherever she shined her spotlight, there was radical change. I wondered what would happen when she got to Yahoo!'s data organization.

As I spent more time in the data organization, I ran into issues. For example, I was the data representative in a war room that was investigating how bids were being gamed in Yahoo!'s display ad exchange. A custom analysis was needed that relied on a data source known for years to be inaccurate, but the hope was that it could still provide some clues or clarity about the theories being discussed in the war room. The results ended up being gibberish. I was also asked to sign off on a new data source that provided details not available in Yahoo!'s standard reporting system. The new data source was inconsistent with Yahoo!'s vetted reporting system by as much as 90 percent; part of this difference could be explained but not all of it. With stakeholder confidence in the data organization already low, I wasn't willing to sign off on it even though the company was in desperate need of more detailed reporting.

One day, a *Harvard Business Review* article titled "Data Scientist: The Sexiest Job of the 21st Century" was circulating. I thought it was a joke, but since it was October, as far away from April Fool's Day as possible, maybe not. To me, my job was so unsexy that I had moved far away and started talking to trees, which made me wonder many times if I had gone insane. I believed that data science had the potential to be sexy if used to create joy and balance in the world, but tech didn't seem to be headed in that direction.

On a positive note, I noticed that my morale at work had improved over the past few months. My boss was a person of high integrity and intelligence. He also trusted the team and let us work from home one day a week. On those days, I was able to sleep in and go for a long walk after work, which made a huge difference. Mayer's leadership lifted my spirits as well. I felt like she had taken charge of the situation at Yahoo! and had a plan to address the problems she'd identified. It was a strong start. In her first quarter at Yahoo!, she had a phenomenal 97 percent approval rating from employees.[8]

At the beginning of Mayer's second quarter, there was a question about layoffs at the weekly all-hands. She replied that there were no present plans for layoffs and that a process for measuring performance would be coming. This was met with applause. Behind the scenes, the board had told her she had to lay off up to half of all employees, but she pushed back, saying that morale was too low, and recommended using a different approach.[9] In the coming weeks, the new process was revealed.

In lieu of layoffs, Yahoo! would start using a stack-ranking system. Every quarter, employees would be rated on a scale of 1 (lowest) to 5 (highest), with a fixed percentage of employees falling into each group. Any employees scoring a 1 for two quarters in a row would be fired. The description of a 1 sounded like someone totally incompetent and, after six rounds of layoffs under previous CEOs, there weren't any 1s in my area. Nonetheless, some employees would be forced into that group under the new system. This didn't sound like a way to help morale.

The failures of stack ranking had been well publicized, notably at Microsoft. Two weeks before Mayer joined Yahoo!, *Vanity Fair* had published an exposé titled "Microsoft's Downfall: Inside the Executive Emails and Cannibalistic Culture That Felled a Tech Giant," which sparked a flurry of follow-up articles from *Forbes, Computerworld, ZDNet, Business Insider*, and other publications. *Vanity Fair*'s Kurt Eichenwald revealed that, "Every current and former Microsoft employee I interviewed—every one—cited stack ranking as the most destructive process inside of Microsoft, something that drove out untold numbers of employees. It leads to employees focusing on competing with each other rather than competing with other companies." His research also highlighted the connection between Microsoft's failure to succeed in the mobile phone market and stack ranking. He interviewed a former Microsoft marketing manager, who said, "You look at the Windows Phone and you can't help but wonder, how did Microsoft squander the lead they had with the Windows CE devices? They had a great lead; they were years ahead. And they completely blew it. And they completely blew it because of the bureaucracy."[10]

Bearing this in mind, and given that one of Mayer's goals was to focus heavily on mobile apps, I wondered why she was choosing to follow in Microsoft's footsteps. Who would benefit from this? I knew that she wasn't an irrational person. My best guess was that stack ranking was being used to get mass numbers of employees to leave Yahoo! without having to pay severance. Layoffs in the form of corporate musical chairs suddenly seemed compassionate. Now we would be playing corporate dodgeball. Employees would be pitted against each other in a drawn-out, aggressive process of elimination: hit others while avoiding being hit.

My intuition told me to leave immediately. My logical self also told me to run for the hills. Then I doubted myself because the people around me didn't show any signs of concern or discontent with the system, only with each other. Were they saying yes to stack ranking out of fear, or did they see something I was missing? I decided to stay and see how things played out.

Some of the stack-ranking criteria started to be revealed. In a staff meeting we were shown a slide with dozens of buzz phrases, like *ruthless prioritization*, that management would be using to assess employee performance. Anyone in the room could have been ranked as a 1 or a 5 depending on which set of attributes management chose to justify their rating. This meant a lot of time and energy would need to be spent managing one's management chain, which was also referenced in the *Vanity Fair* article.

I thought about submitting an all-hands question asking why Yahoo! switched to stack ranking in light of the results at Microsoft, but I lacked confidence and was afraid of sounding defiant. Instead, I submitted a question about whether the stack-ranking process would penalize employees for working on innovative projects which didn't pan out. I wanted to get a sense of Mayer's philosophy on taking risks. My question got the second highest number of votes that week.

Mayer responded by saying that she would personally reward taking risks that had high potential, but ultimately it would be up to each employee's management chain to decide. She recommended getting approval from management before taking risks. That sounded like a reasonable approach in theory, but in practice it would be slow and cumbersome to get approval and upper management could still penalize employees at their discretion with no recourse. My impression was that employees' immediate bosses wouldn't have much say in the rating and the decisions would be made higher up the chain. When it came down to it, I realized that I didn't trust those people to support me in a subjective rating system, nor did I have any desire to become a schmoozer.

More ways to weed out employees were brought forth. At one all-hands, Mayer invited employees who had been at Yahoo! for more than five years to leave. She was clear that we weren't being fired and it was just a suggestion to get experience elsewhere in the industry. She said that her staff would even help us find jobs and we could always re-apply to Yahoo! in the future. It was true that getting a fresh perspective was a good thing, and I'd received a similar message during my job search: "Why have you been at Yahoo! for six years? That's such a long time," followed by an eye roll. Hearing it from Mayer, though, surprised me. She had been at Google for thirteen years right before coming to Yahoo!. This felt like another attempt to get employees to leave without having to pay their severance.

The dials were turned up further as change to the company culture accelerated. The cafeteria began serving dinner, like Google did. Almost nobody showed up, and Mayer expressed her disappointment with us. The effects of stack ranking began to kick in, with more noticeable tension and finger-pointing at meetings. Employees were feeling the pressure being evaluated quarterly with stack ranking instead of annually as it had been previously. For instance, taking a vacation would put someone at a disadvantage for the quarter. There was no downtime built into the process, and it felt unsustainable.

I went to the redwoods to sort things out. When I visited my tree, the first thing that came up was "tree rings." I remembered learning in elementary school that a tree trunk consisted of concentric rings, each representing a year in the tree's life. My simplistic recollection was that thicker rings indicated a higher growth year due to factors such as rainfall, temperature, and the age of the tree. Also, each ring usually consisted of a thin, dark-colored portion that formed during the colder parts of the year with less sunlight and a thick, light-colored portion that formed during the warmer parts of the year with more sunlight.

I then thought about how Yahoo! was switching from annual cycles to quarterly cycles, like seasons. The problem was that Yahoo! wanted every season to be summer. If employees were trees, our tree rings would need to be monochromatic, of the lightest color, and resembling a single, massive mutant ring. I sensed that this would result in a shorter lifespan, and I felt sick. I remembered receiving a similar message about the lack of cycles in the online world during my experimentation with the oracle cards.

Feeling into the tree, I could envision the yin and yang (dark and light) of each of its rings from the inside out and its necessity for the tree's longevity. I understood that Silicon Valley was rejecting the yin feminine energy and, with it, balance. I had to remind myself that just because Mayer was female, it didn't mean she embraced feminine energy. She operated with masculine dynamics in the workplace and expected the same from the rest of us.

Then I thought about how I was experiencing a similar but opposite problem in my apartment complex. A neighbor unbalanced the complex by rejecting yang masculine energy.

She pretended to be helpless to manipulate people into doing things for her and then played the victim when she didn't get her way. The entire complex revolved around her needs because she would report people to the landlord or spread gossip about anyone who didn't cooperate.

When I first moved in, she approached me in the driveway, asked a lot of personal questions, complained about all the men in the complex as well as the landlord, cried while telling me that she was an old woman living alone, and then asked for my phone number. She didn't look that old, and it turned out that she wasn't much older than me. I suggested that she could probably find a roommate easily, and she snapped at me, "I don't want to live with anyone!"

One day, someone from the next block parked their truck in front of our building. A few hours later, they received a parking ticket because my neighbor called the sheriff's office and reported that the truck had been there for more than three days, which was the legal limit. She told me she wanted to reserve the spot for a van pick up the next day and didn't leave a note or try talking to the truck owner because she didn't like conflict. When I pointed out that she was the one who caused the conflict, she ignored me and changed the subject to how hard life is and began crying. She didn't express any remorse for lying to the sheriff. One of the other neighbors summed up the incident by saying, "The black hole strikes again."

My neighbor's behavior felt like feminine energy gone wrong, just as the dynamics at Yahoo! and in the online world felt like masculine energy gone wrong. I didn't want to lose sight of the positive feminine and masculine energies in my life, so I made a quick-and-dirty grid to summarize what I was experiencing, illustrated in Figure 1 below. On one axis were the complementary feminine and masculine energies, and on the other axis were the polarities of these energies. I reminded myself that masculine and feminine energy didn't correspond to gender and that everyone embodied aspects of both. My best friend was a wonderful example of embodying both energies in a healthy way. I saw aspects of myself in all four quadrants.

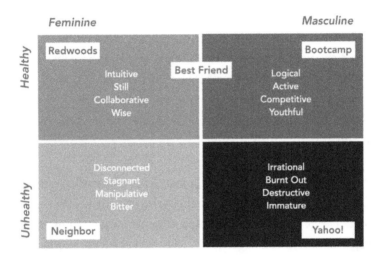

Figure 1. My Experience in Balancing Masculine and Feminine Energy in 2013

The grid helped me see how I achieved a greater sense of balance in my life. For instance, when I was feeling burnt out (unhealthy masculine), I gravitated toward stillness (healthy feminine), such as meditating, napping, or communing with my redwood tree.

What stood out to me in the grid was the childish, destructive dynamic at Yahoo!. One possible solution to restore balance would be to infuse Yahoo! with positive feminine energy, specifically maternal energy. In the physical world, our planet is sometimes referred to as Mother Earth, and I wished for a similar concept in the online world. I remembered wondering what Jerry Yang's mother thought of Microsoft's offer to buy Yahoo!. It felt like adult supervision was needed to help Microsoft "play well with others," and it felt like adult supervision was needed now to prevent Yahoo! from turning into Microsoft.

Things at work were becoming even more tense. Mayer expected employees to discuss ideas for turning the company around with each other, but why would we? If two people came up with an idea to save the company, only one of them could receive a 5 in the stack-ranking system. Employees ended up sitting in their cubes with headphones on, not talking to each other. I started seeing people crying in conference rooms, and I was feeling frustrated myself. The last straw was that there was talk of an upcoming company-wide policy banning working from home so that we could all collaborate and innovate even more!

It was obvious that Yahoo! was not headed for the big turnaround everyone had been hoping for. I dreaded going into work each day, and I had been saving as much money as possible since the 2008 stock market crash. I was also aching to spend more time at home exploring the coast. I knew the timing was right for me to resign, and so I handed in my notice.

Shortly afterwards, the official announcement banning Yahoo! employees from working from home made national headlines. All staff had to be in a Yahoo! office five days a week, with mandatory core hours between 9 a.m. and 5 p.m., subjecting them to the worst of the traffic on their commute. Those who didn't live near a Yahoo! office had ninety days to relocate or leave. Employees were told that working from home had been abused. My boss assured the team that he didn't feel that way about us, but the lack of trust from the highest levels was clear. It felt like the priority was to treat all employees as though they were irresponsible rather than focusing on helping the top employees thrive.

At the next all-hands, nearly every question was about the work-from-home ban. Mayer made a general statement that she thought having everyone in the office was what Yahoo! needed right now. She didn't elaborate or acknowledge the impact it was having the lives of employees.

When I made my rounds to say goodbye during my last week, I was surprised by some of the reactions. Three service employees in three different locations on campus smiled and talked to me through their teeth like ventriloquists. They each started off with, "Is anybody watching?" I gathered that they weren't allowed to chat. One person opened up and said there were new rules for service employees, including no longer being able to use the main elevators; they had been relegated to the freight elevators. I was tremendously saddened.

When I left, I didn't know what was to come next for me. I just knew I needed to rest. I found that after seven years of working at Yahoo! I was out of touch with everyday life. For instance, I was shocked to see so many people in the supermarket in the middle of the day on weekdays. There was an entire world oblivious to cubicles and corporate goals. It took time to adjust. Initially, I was upset to find out that Mayer's 2012 compensation for her first six months at Yahoo! was $36.6 million while I had no income. Then I realized I wouldn't want to trade places.

Snippets of information trickled in about what happened at Yahoo! after my departure, and all of it validated my decision to leave, deepening my confidence in my intuition. Co-workers told me I was lucky to go when I did because things got very ugly. Our organization was given the option to remain under one of the higher level leaders I didn't trust, and almost every single person chose to leave. A *New York Times* article sent to me by my eye doctor (who has a fascination with tech culture) stated that, during Yahoo!'s quarterly calibration meetings, "managers would use these meetings to conjure reasons that certain staff members should get negative reviews. Sometimes the reason would be political or superficial." It reported that employees didn't want to work together because only so many top ratings could be given in the stack-ranking process. Employees ended up asking for an all-hands dedicated to answering questions about stack ranking and if the questions could be submitted anonymously.[11]

As time went on, things got even worse at Yahoo!. In 2015, more than a third of employees left the company voluntarily or involuntarily. In 2016, Verizon bought Yahoo! for $4.83 billion and then reduced the price by $350 million due to two record-breaking data breaches announced after the purchase. This put the price at about 10 percent of what Microsoft had offered to buy Yahoo! in 2008. In 2017, Mayer was declared the least likable CEO in tech. A couple of weeks later, she left Yahoo! And, between her shares and severance pay, ended up departing with $260 million in compensation. A few months later, it was revealed that one of the record-breaking data breaches was understated. Instead of one billion accounts hacked, it was all three billion Yahoo! accounts. As of 2023, this is still the biggest data breach in history.

Yahoo! went out with a bang, no pun intended. Meanwhile, I was still standing, with a notch on my trunk, seven rings wider, and ready for whatever came next.

CHAPTER 3
RESPONSIBILITY

When I joined GoPro's Data Science and Engineering team in February 2015, it felt like a dream job. I loved the brand, the job description, the team, and the CEO's vision. GoPro's outlook was strong, and I had many ideas for using data to help the company succeed.

GoPro was founded in 2002 by CEO Nick Woodman, borne from his desire to take photos while surfing. There were no consumer action cameras at the time, so he decided to invent his own. Woodman and his wife sold shell jewelry and belts from their VW van to raise money for the venture, but most of the funding came from his parents. In 2005, when GoPro released a small film camera in a waterproof case with a wrist strap, the surfing selfie was born. The following year, the company launched a digital version of the camera named Digital HERO.

Over time, GoPro developed camera mounts and other accessories to capture new perspectives from a variety of action sports as well as everyday life. For instance, GoPro offered handlebar mounts for bikers and cyclists, and dog harnesses to see life from a dog's point of view. In 2010, GoPro launched their next generation of action camera, named HD HERO due to its high-definition resolution, and referred to the product line as HERO for simplicity.

My love of the GoPro brand began in 2012 when my best friend and I started using the HERO2 on our motorcycle adventures. True to its name, the camera helped me access my bolder side. We experimented with different mounts, camera angles, and settings to get the most compelling shots. My favorite capture was a Van Gogh-esque motion blur in the redwoods that resembled a swirling, timbered reverie.

I got goosebumps when my best friend announced one day that GoPro had opened an office nearby. I was still working at Yahoo! and had fantasized about leaving my job to join GoPro. Woodman openly attributed his success with GoPro to his intuition, which was refreshing to me, as was the concept of technology that inspired people to be outdoors. I certainly wanted to spend more time surfing waves instead of surfing the web. I walked over to the GoPro office and submitted my résumé but was told that it would be a while before they had data positions and to keep checking.

When I left Yahoo!, I didn't see any data openings listed on GoPro's website. I explored potential career changes, but I wasn't able to find the right fit. For example, I applied to non-profits seeking to use data for positive change in the world, but the pay was generally too low. I also thought about going back to school for a new degree, but I wasn't sufficiently drawn to a profession to justify years of evenings and weekends doing coursework. The truth was that I enjoyed working with data. I just didn't like how it was being applied in the tech industry. I kept looking for an acceptable tradeoff between purpose and pay.

Fast-forward to 2014 and GoPro was riding a huge wave of

success. In June, they went public; in September, they released the HERO4 camera with an electrifying launch video, "GoPro HERO4: The Adventure of Life in 4K"; and, by the end of the year, Woodman was the highest paid CEO in America. After viewing GoPro's launch video at BestBuy, I began watching the full series on YouTube. In between swear words, the narrator of the first video, "GoPro: Descent into the Lava of Marum in 4K," described the agony and the ecstasy of the deepest ever descent into the active volcano located in the Republic of Vanuatu. The grand finale of Geoff Mackley beholding the unfathomably colossal primeval sea of palpitating magma left my heart pounding. I was in complete awe.

I immediately checked GoPro's career page. They had moved to a bigger office twenty minutes away and were hiring for many positions, including data analysts! I sent multiple applications, but they were rejected. I suspected that being more than forty years old was a contributing factor. Data modeling, like super modeling, was a vocation strictly for the young, with few exceptions.

Fortuitously, an impromptu fairy god-crew helped me get my foot in the door. At the time, I was a visitor services volunteer at Point Reyes National Seashore (PRNS), where one of the rangers recommended that I watch *The Internship*, a comedy about two laid-off salesmen in their forties who land summer internships at Google. The movie helped me stay optimistic and gave me some ideas for playing up my experience. A volunteer at the PRNS gift shop encouraged me to apply for the jobs I really wanted, even if I didn't meet all the qualifications. Lastly, my eye doctor gave me some pointers for writing an effective cover letter and recommended removing my earliest jobs from my résumé so my age wasn't as obvious.

Success! The day after I submitted my résumé and cover letter for a new position at GoPro, which I really wanted but didn't meet all the criteria for, I was contacted for an initial phone screening and then invited to interview in person.

My experience during the interview process was mixed. Most of the panel members were welcoming and engaging. One person, however, barely made eye contact from the get-go and cautiously held my résumé from the top corners, as though it were covered with a contagious disease. Another person walked into the room, looked at me, and immediately rolled his eyes before saying hello. I was asked twice if I had been laid off from my previous job—I said no and then was asked if I was sure, which meant they thought I was lying. I was told to prepare a project, on which I spent a significant amount of time, but nobody requested to see it. I shared it anyway for practice. I was used to these types of experiences at tech interviews and knew I wouldn't be getting the job.

A couple of weeks later, the head of the GoPro Data Science and Engineering (DSE), who had been part of the interview panel, reached out to see if I wanted to interview for an upcoming role in his team. They had just built GoPro's first data platform (a data platform is integrated technology for an organization's end-to-end data needs) using Cloudera (Cloudera is the vendor co-founded by the leader of the PIE team I was part of at Yahoo!). They were looking for another architect to design the ingestion of new data sources onto GoPro's data platform, create reference documentation, and train end users. The main goal was for me to empower data analysts. It sounded like an incredible opportunity, and we arranged a round of onsite interviews.

The DSE team was mostly former Apple employees. They had already started using the data platform to improve consumer product and marketing experiences. For example, the HERO's default resolution was changed to better match the way people were using the camera, based on the activity data in the platform.

During the interviews I was struck by the team's chemistry. They seemed authentically happy and spoke affectionately of each other and their work. The time flew by, a positive sign. The main challenge the team faced was that a number of key decision-makers in the company, including Woodman, were not data-driven and relied purely on intuition. This meant that DSE was a small team and low on the organizational chart. Part of the job would be to evangelize the new data platform to decision-makers so DSE could expand and have influence. I was concerned by this, but if any team had the talent and showmanship to pull it off, it was this one. Helping the data analysts succeed would be an important part of making the case.

I felt that this job had enormous potential for using data to support intuitive innovation. Unlike the web's advertising revenue model, which was free for consumers, GoPro's revenue came predominantly from consumers. If the cameras weren't simple, easy, and fun to use, people wouldn't buy them. GoPro had no choice but to respect consumers' time and quality of experience, which resonated with me.

After a few more rounds of interviews, I was thrilled to receive an offer. On my first day, my boss gave me a tour of the office and I heard laughter and the vibrant hum of productivity. The DSE lab was hopping with stakeholders who were working, testing products, and hanging out. It had been so long since I was in a healthy work environment that I was shocked by the camaraderie.

On the second day was a "family hang," GoPro's moniker for their company-wide all-hands, which took place in the "Experience Room" filled with high-adrenaline images and gadgets. The company had a phenomenal quarter and people were euphoric. Woodman expressed immense gratitude for his journey, acknowledging that it had been a "shit show" at times, and shared his vision for the future, which included producing original content and simplifying editing and sharing camera footage via the GoPro mobile app. He also announced that every Thursday employees would have a three-hour lunch (called Live It, Love It, Eat It) to go out, explore, and use the products. He encouraged us to be as creative as possible. The room exploded with cheers and applause. After the meeting, my boss introduced me to Woodman, who was immensely welcoming and down to earth. He chatted with us for more than fifteen minutes. I was buzzing for days afterwards!

Every week I looked forward to Live It, Love It, Eat It. One Thursday, I invited DSE to my neighborhood. Another time, I toured a plant nursery owned by one of the Point Reyes National Seashore volunteers. She recommended that I visit a nearby historic estate to see their magnificent flower arrangements. The following Thursday, I went to the estate and a sweet guy with a GoPro mounted on his chest saw my HERO4 and asked if I was a GoPro employee too. We decided to explore the estate together and began meeting every week for Live It, Love It, Eat It. We hunted for mushrooms in the redwoods, explored a shell beach at the bay, hiked, played pool, and returned often to the estate to see the rotating gardens. Eventually we became significant others.

While I loved my job and looked forward to going into the office, it was clear from day one that the exhilaration might be short-lived. At Yahoo!, there were several hundred people on the data team. At GoPro, there were fewer than ten. We needed to grow substantially or there would be problems ahead. The bigger issue was how far down the organizational chart we were. When I left Yahoo!, the head of the data team reported directly to the CEO. At GoPro, the head of DSE was several levels down from the CEO and was pushed down another level the week I joined. He began reporting to a vice president who had no background in data and never met with the team to learn more.

For a while, though, work went smoothly. A couple of people joined our team, and we were adding new data sources to the state-of-the-art platform at record speed. Analysts started building dashboards and gleaning insights. After a few months, we did an office-wide presentation of DSE's services, capabilities, and successes about thirty feet from our vice president's office, yet he did not bother to attend. Soon after, the vice president pushed DSE down another level in the organizational chart by inserting a senior director between us.

The head of DSE requested additional employees in anticipation of supporting GoPro's biggest software release ever as well as the steadily increasing demand from stakeholder teams, which were growing both in size and sophistication. The heads of the stakeholder and analyst teams also submitted requests to upper management for additional DSE employees to ensure their needs would be met. The requests were denied, and, as far I was aware, no reason was given.

The scope of my job had blown up, and I was feeling the impact. In addition to the growing data work, about half of my job became quality assurance. A quality assurance team was supposed to provide support for the DSE team, but they were also chronically understaffed.

Meanwhile, the company released Session, a simpler-to-use camera in its HERO4 line aimed at mainstream consumers. To celebrate, the company rented out Great America amusement park for the employees. Unfortunately, like the park's famed Drop Tower free-fall ride, GoPro's success was about to plummet at a stomach-turning pace. Employees at all levels had warned Woodman about the risks of the unconventional timing of Session's release on July 6 (as opposed to a couple of months before the end-of-year holidays or the start of summer) and the high price of $399 not providing value for money. Woodman took ownership of the timing and price, saying that he had followed his intuition. Due to slow sales, GoPro ended up dropping the price of Session twice, by $100 each time. By the end of 2015, GoPro shares fell by 70 percent for the year,[1] while the Nasdaq Composite Index was up by 6 percent.[2]

GoPro started 2016 by laying off 7 percent of its workforce.[3] It also publicly announced it was planning to launch several new products and services later in the year, such as GoPro's first drone, the HERO5 camera, a content management product, mobile app editing, and a cloud subscription service that would reduce the time from capture to sharing. On CNBC's *Squawk on the Street*, Woodman declared, "2016 is the single most exciting year for new products that we've ever had at GoPro. Whether it's hardware, software, entertainment products that we're developing, this is the biggest year ever for GoPro."[4]

There was immediate internal backlash because it was obvious there were far too few employees to deliver everything promised in time for the 2016 holiday season. Political fighting ensued as teams competed for resources. The demands on the DSE team increased several fold as new data pipelines needed to be built for most of the upcoming products and services. Stakeholders offered to pay for new DSE employees with their own budget but continued to encounter roadblocks from upper management, again with no reason given as far I was aware.

The head of DSE left, which felt like the beginning of the end. He had been a fantastic, award-winning leader who built the team from scratch, and my experience taught me that the team would likely disband after his departure.

My gut told me to resign. I knew that the company's goals were wildly unrealistic and that our team was particularly unsupported by senior leadership. DSE's reputation was suffering in the process because we weren't able to meet stakeholders' expectations. However, I stayed because I had been at GoPro for only a year and didn't feel I had enough of a financial cushion to walk away. I struggled with the practical need for a paycheck versus staying in a negligent, dysfunctional workplace where we were set up to fail.

Wasn't GoPro obligated to shareholders to do their best to deliver the publicly-announced products on schedule? Didn't Woodman have a fundamental desire for the business to succeed? Perhaps he still hadn't made the transition from operating as a private business, where he answered to his parents and a handful of investors, to a public one, where he answered to a large number of institutional, individual, and internal shareholders. A class action lawsuit had been filed against GoPro in January 2016 to try to recoup investor losses from the Session, but that didn't appear to serve as a wakeup call to operate differently.

When engineers made errors or used poor judgment that significantly impacted the business, they had to perform a root cause analysis (RCA) to identify who/what caused a problem, the impact it had, how it was fixed, and how it will be prevented from reoccurring. Depending on the findings, an RCA could result in the termination of one or more employees. Executives seemed exempt from this type of internal accountability, which felt frustrating.

Soon I began having crippling headaches and crying uncontrollably, a first in my life. I often had to lie down in a quiet place to cope and became socially withdrawn. Every single workday I had to talk myself into going into the office, and then I had to talk myself into getting out of the car once I got there. I began eating more junk food and shopping online.

When I got home from work, I just wanted to be alone. Unfortunately, my "black hole" neighbor often approached me with some type of complaint as I walked from my parking spot to my apartment. She often put her clutter in places it didn't belong and felt wronged when it didn't work out. One time she decided to store items in the garage of a recently-deceased tenant and was upset when the unit was rented. "I can't believe this is happening to me!" she exclaimed tearfully, without taking any personal responsibility. When I pointed out that we each had a storage closet in our garages, she said she couldn't fit another thing in hers and, with a straight face, blamed her small dog. Early on, she had encroached into my space while I was on a vacation, and when I called her out on it she retorted, "I thought you weren't coming back!" and then cackled and scurried away. I found her shamelessness and lack of boundaries disturbing. I changed the time I came home from work in hopes of avoiding her.

I remembered to turn to nature for comfort and began sitting in front of the ocean on a regular basis. My situation at GoPro felt like I had been swept away by a rip current. One moment everything was pleasant and the next I found myself dangerously far from where I started and in a panic. I recalled that the way out of a rip current is to swim parallel to shore and then proceed diagonally back so as not to end up in the current again. I had tried going against the powerful current of my work situation and was exhausted. I wondered what the equivalent of swimming parallel to shore and then diagonally back would look like? I would soon find out.

One day, my best friend asked how I was doing and I broke down in tears. I told him about my job, and he recommended that I call GoPro's employee assistance program (EAP) to consult with a professional since I wasn't able to give myself permission to resign. I followed his advice in baby steps. First, I found EAP's phone number in my benefits materials. The next day, I dialed the number and was approved for three free sessions with a therapist. The day after that, I made an appointment with the therapist. Within a week, I was face to face with someone who could help me.

The therapist was highly efficient in sorting out my situation. He assessed that I was experiencing major depression caused by my job, that my job situation was beyond my control to change and had no signs of improving, and that I had enough savings to cover my expenses until I could find another job. He recommended that I resign, and I felt tremendous relief and validation. One of the other options would have been to start taking antidepressants, but that crossed a line for me. I didn't want to have to take drugs in order to do my job.

A few days later, I submitted my resignation, letting my boss know I loved the team but couldn't handle the situation that upper management had put us in. I told him about my depression symptoms, which I had been too embarrassed to mention before, and the outcome of my session with the EAP therapist. I mentioned that I felt like I was crazy because nobody on the team had been talking about the obvious problems we were facing and that the situation felt hopeless since high-level stakeholders had been advocating for us with no luck. My boss was incredibly supportive and let me know confidentially that he was close to resigning as well. He said that I wasn't crazy and asked if I would be open to hearing some options for staying. I agreed.

To my surprise, the next morning the senior director was waiting to meet me and my boss in person. The senior director worked out of a different office, and it was a long commute for him to the headquarters. The three of us had a frank conversation about upper management's lack of availability and support for DSE. I was perversely consoled to learn that other teams in my division were treated similarly. I was also informed that a new DSE director had been hired, though he wouldn't be joining for a while. The outcome of the meeting was that I would take time off while my boss and the senior director worked on hiring an additional employee. I was deeply grateful for their efforts to retain me.

While I was away, my depression symptoms subsided and I felt like my old self again. My boss contacted me to say that he had resigned but would still be at work when I returned. I was saddened that the architecture team was coming to an end. I reflected on how much we had accomplished while having fun and learning from each other, a rare experience in the corporate world. Under the circumstances, the process of hiring someone new for the team was paused, which meant the team was shrinking instead of growing.

When I returned to work, several people commented on how much happier and relaxed I looked. In contrast, most of DSE team looked despondent. While I was gone, one of the stakeholder teams lent DSE a talented data scientist to temporarily help out with our lack of staff and they already looked despondent too. It felt futile; we needed much more than just one extra person to turn things around;.

One morning, a few of us were gazing out the window when someone from the team almost got hit by a car as he walked zombie-like toward the office. We were yelling at him to get out the way, but obviously he couldn't hear us and just kept walking. Although it wasn't a laughing matter, we later teased him about his catatonic state, and the and the team finally started talking about the toll our situation was taking on us.

A few days later, DSE's system administrator resigned, which was a critical loss. We'd gone from a skeleton crew to a few scattered bones. Management hadn't assigned anyone to take over the system administrator's duties, and it didn't take long after he left to realize that nobody had the password to the data platform, let alone training on its configuration and maintenance. After the absurdity of our circumstances sank in, all we could do was laugh.

In a positive development, the senior director began doing the long commute to sit with our team a few times a week, stabilizing our situation. The project manager led daily meetings, bringing structure and normalcy to the workday. They both set expectations with stakeholders, reducing incoming requests. Still, it was difficult to overcome the glaring lack of resources. It was going to be a while before the DSE director could start, nobody else had joined, and we continued to have no quality assurance support after six months of waiting. My headaches returned.

At this point, much of the company was in anarchy. There had been a mass exodus of employees, and those who remained had become increasingly overwhelmed and rebellious. I started hearing more four-letter words at meetings and realized I was becoming impatient and short with people. A few times a day, I went to an empty room and sat on the floor, resting my head on my knees. I saw other employees doing the same or sitting with their backs against the wall, staring into space. I felt frustrated that employees had no recourse other than to leave.

I wondered again why Woodman was letting his ship sink. He was a brilliant innovator, but when it came to staffing and organizing to deliver, the company continued to be stuck in "shit show" mode. When I looked more closely, I saw that, for better or worse, Woodman was operating in relative isolation.

He was GoPro's founder, CEO, chairman of the board, and top shareholder with 77 percent of the voting power.[5] He had taken on an extraordinary level of responsibility when the company went public. Perhaps if there had been more distribution of power, such as someone else being chairman of the board, things would have gone more smoothly. I also wondered if some of his decisions had been impulsive rather than intuitive. Both are "thoughtless" approaches to decision-making, but the former comes from being disconnected while the latter taps into what you feel deep inside.

I continued to visit the ocean on a regular basis to feel more centered. I thought back to visiting the redwoods, which taught me to endure the decline at Yahoo!. Now I was drawn to the ocean and watching birds and whales migrate. When it came to fight or flight, the ocean wildlife was teaching me flight, which seemed like the appropriate survival strategy for dealing with GoPro's impending crash. I googled the animal with the longest migration path and found that the arctic tern flies more than a million miles in its lifetime, with annual round trips between the northern arctic circle and Antarctica. Arctic terns are able to achieve this feat by gliding with air currents above the ocean in pursuit of sunlight and fish.

When I imagined myself effortlessly taking flight to another job with favorable conditions, the word *flighty* popped into my mind. According to the *Cambridge Dictionary*, *flighty* means "(especially of a woman) not responsible and likely to change activities, jobs, boyfriends, etc."[6] I was reminded that our culture has a negative view of women who take flight, even when fleeing from harmful situations. When men change jobs they are considered ambitious, and when they change girlfriends they are studs. I didn't care if anyone thought I was flighty. My depression symptoms were becoming more intense, and I knew what I had to do.

I resigned again. This time, the senior director asked me to hold on for two more weeks because the DSE director would be arriving and bringing someone with him who would assist with my projects. I initially resisted, but agreed to stay.

The DSE director arrived, overflowing with enthusiasm, and seemed like a very nice person. He articulated great plans for the team and was excited to jump in. It was obvious from the way he spoke, however, that he had not been fully informed of the situation he'd signed up for. Furthermore, nobody came with him to assist with my projects. The director said that the new employee would be arriving in September, three months away and after most of my projects were due.

The following week, I resigned for a third time, as did the two data engineers I worked most closely with. I didn't know they would be resigning, but I wasn't surprised. The new director was blindsided and asked if time off would help. I told him that I had already taken time off and filled him in on the team's situation. After the shock wore off, he mentioned that he had sold his house and moved for this job. I felt badly for him.

When I announced my departure more broadly, I was open about leaving due to burnout. The DSE member who had almost been hit by a car asked if I thought he might be burned out. I looked at him. His hair was disheveled, he barely blinked, he talked more slowly than usual, and his shoulders were hunched over. I responded with a resounding "Yes!"

I sent my goodbye email to a wide distribution list. I received many responses, including from the chief product officer and chief information officer, but not a single person in my management chain acknowledged my departure other than the new DSE director. Several people asked me to high-light in my exit interview how the role of the vice president was disastrous for data stakeholders across the company, which I did. A couple of co-workers commented that they wished they had the freedom to leave too but needed to have a job lined up first to support their family and pay their mortgage. I wondered how they had the energy to take care of their children in the evenings, let alone search for a new job.

After my last day, it took a couple of months for me to feel normal again. Like the aftermath of a bad breakup, I cleared my apartment of everything that reminded me of GoPro, including all my HEROs. I kept cycling through the stages of grief: denial, anger, bargaining, depression, and acceptance. I read self-help books, slept deeply, and meditated frequently. When I felt better, I decided to take a solo road trip to reflect on my time at GoPro and figure out what came next.

I thought about how I might have handled things differently with the benefit of hindsight. I would have left GoPro sooner. I would have communicated my struggles to my boss earlier on. When I looked deeper, I saw that I wouldn't have joined GoPro at all.

Before I received my job offer from GoPro, I was making progress on a Science on a Sphere (SOS) presentation at Point Reyes National Seashore. SOS is a data visualization system created by the National Oceanic and Atmospheric Administration to help audiences gain insight into Earth's environmental processes. The system projects planetary data onto a six-foot-wide carbon fiber sphere hanging from the ceiling. When the ranger who had trained me over the years said I was ready to do SOS, I was ecstatic! It was the ideal data insights opportunity for me, but unpaid. With hundreds of SOS datasets to choose from, I wrote a first draft script about balancing land usage as the Earth's population increases over time to accommodate evolving agriculture, urban development, and wildlife/wilderness preservation needs.

The job offer from GoPro came right after I reviewed the

script with the ranger, and I had to make a decision quickly. My intuition told me not to accept the offer and keep working on my SOS script while continuing my job search. My logical mind pointed out that I needed a paycheck and had been searching for a job for six months already. It also reasoned that GoPro seemed like an excellent fit and was a place I had been excited about for a few years. With GoPro now behind me, I couldn't help but wonder how things would have turned out if I had followed my intuition. I imagined I would have been poorer but much happier.

I thought about the cumulative impact on my mental health and relationships from years of choosing to work in culturally toxic corporate environments. I had become an isolated, tired person. The job searches alone drained me. Between the two teams at GoPro, I did eighteen interviews and a project, not to mention the many interviews and projects with other non-profit, government, education, and tech organizations. I didn't know if I had the energy to go through another round, and I didn't feel equipped to handle another extreme work situation should I encounter one.

I recognized that I no longer had a career so much as a life of solo, itinerant employment. Thinking about my happiest friends, I realized they weren't in the tech industry. I wanted to start choosing differently, but I didn't know how to go about it.

I had a sudden desire to re-watch the "Descent into the Lava of Marum" video I had been so captivated by nearly two years earlier. Glimpsing into the fiery, miraculous depths of the planet, I experienced the same primal stirring and awe. This time, I focused on Geoff Mackley's narration: "Mother Nature is always doing something to restore balance." I had the epiphany that I needed to look into the fiery, miraculous depths of myself instead of living disconnectedly and wearily at the surface. I pictured magma bubbling and tossing inside of me, awaiting form, and then felt a spark of life in my body. The splitting headaches and uncontrollable tears, I realized, were from my inner volcano relieving pressure and restoring balance by forcing me to step away from damaging, extreme conditions. I wondered how Mother Nature had been restoring the balance of GoPro's leadership and what they would see if they faced their inner magma.

I started to view my time at GoPro with more appreciation. I cherished the phenomenal times I had at the beginning of the job and began to see the gifts of the challenging times. I had more clarity on where I drew the line between earning a living versus working in an unhealthy environment. I was more conscious of burnout and the need to prioritize self-care. I felt more open and willing to follow my heart rather than derail myself with fear. I had connected with my colleagues on a deeper, more meaningful level. I got to witness the inner workings of a brand I had loved. I pictured how data could be used to set up GoPro for success and recalled the joy of solving puzzles again. I learned that balance was incredibly important to me. I got a chance to use my voice. I discovered that I was surrounded by helpful people. I experienced that not using data at all could be as harmful as misusing data—invaluable wisdom for my career.

By the last day of my road trip I felt much more relaxed and at peace, but I didn't know what my next step would be. As I was driving south on the Avenue of the Giants in northern California, I witnessed a display of magnificent light beams, ethereally reflecting the mist of the redwood forest. I pulled over, ran into the woods, and stood in the center of one of the otherworldly rays that had a rainbow orb. I asked for a sign of my next step. The first thing that popped into my head was a self-help article I had bookmarked. I reread the article, and then it occurred to me to google the author's name. I discovered that she was offering an eight-month coaching program starting in a few days' time. By the end of the week, I had enrolled and was off on a new path.

The program turned out to be exactly what I needed. It equipped me with tools for creating a happier life for myself, including ways to manage stress. Perhaps the most revelatory part of the experience stemmed from the fact that 97 percent of the participants were female. Going from a male-dominated environment to a female-dominated one made me realize how much energy I had been spending adjusting to a highly masculine way of getting things done. No wonder I had burned out. I imagined how frustrated and impatient some of the macho employees at GoPro would have been in the coaching program where the only f-word used was "feelings."

A couple of weeks after the program started, GoPro announced their product releases for the fourth quarter of 2016. This included GoPro's first drone, named Karma, and the HERO5 camera. At the beginning of November, GoPro announced that there were production issues with Karma and HERO5 and anticipated that they wouldn't be able to meet demand. A few days later, I saw a TV news story that GoPro had recalled Karma because the battery became disconnected mid-flight, causing it to fall from the sky.

I let this sink in:

GoPro's Karma fell from the sky!

The leadership's disconnection from everyone around them had manifested as a battery disconnection in their Karma. It sounded like a movie plot, and I won't deny that it felt incredibly validating. To top it off, the Karma recall occurred on the same day as the United States presidential election. It felt like the political system's karma had fallen from the sky too. A couple of weeks later, a shareholder class action lawsuit was filed, alleging that GoPro's public statements about the Karma release were "materially false and misleading."[7]

At the end of November, GoPro announced that it was closing its entertainment division and laying off 15 percent of its workforce, a third of whom were vice president level and above.[8] Among them was the person from my first round of interviews who had asked me twice if I had been laid off. The vice president of my organization, however, survived the cull and ended up overseeing a larger portion of the company. By the end of 2016, GoPro shares fell by 52 percent for the year,[9] while the Nasdaq Composite Index was up by 8 percent.[10] The stock price had dipped into the single digits and was down more than 90 percent from its all-time high.[11] It was a losing situation for everyone involved, except for the vice president perhaps.

I found myself mapping out how I would use my experience and the tools I had gained to address the pain points of the tech industry. There was always an option to create more joy in the world rather than maximize profits, and to operate collaboratively rather than at the expense of others. I decided to create my own coaching business to explore this further and named it Data for Joy.

CHAPTER 4
LISTENING

I didn't know how to start a business nor did I know what my role might be in advancing the use of data for joy, but action steps began coming to me spontaneously that led me in the right direction. I offered a class for managing work-related stress that I wished had been available to me when I was at GoPro. I also signed up for a variety of nature-connection, self-development, and business courses.

My creative process involved doing a daily "sit spot," a practice mentioned in the multiple courses I was taking. According to the conservation organization Wildsight, "a sit spot is simply a favorite place in nature (or looking out a window at nature) that is visited regularly to cultivate awareness, expand senses, and study patterns of local plants, birds, trees, and animals. The practice supports mindfulness, builds routine, and increases focus."[1]When I first heard about sit spots, I felt like I had found a piece of myself. My regular visits to the redwoods and ocean had a name, there were people I could share my experiences with, and there were new techniques I could try.

Sharing at nature-connection gatherings involved sitting in a circle led by a moderator who set the ground rules for a judgment-free safe zone. We were guided to "hold space" for each other, which meant "being willing to walk alongside another person in whatever journey they [were] on, without judging them, making them feel inadequate, trying to fix them, or trying to impact the outcome."[2] It was about empathetic listening. As people's trust in the circle grew, we shared more deeply and began connecting with each other, like the redwood trees we were surrounded by. *Be like a tree to set someone free,* I thought.

When I returned home after these interactions, the contrast felt harsh. I would turn on the news and see weary-looking analysts dissecting the latest blast of political tweets, especially deleted ones. Listening felt jarring and cacophonous. I lost ten minutes of my life watching a roundtable discussion on what the typo "covfefe" might mean, and this was my wakeup call to consume less news. I felt disheartened that technology enabled the dizzying pace of events, and I wished for solutions.

One day during my sit spot, I received the idea to read more about biomimicry, a subject I had come across when I started communicating with my special redwood tree several years earlier. According to the Biomimicry Institute, "biomimicry is a practice that learns from and mimics the strategies found in nature to solve human design challenges."[3] For example, scientists developed adhesives to close wounds without stitches by emulating the design of gecko toes. Imitating nature's survival strategies had helped me cope with workplace stress at Yahoo! and GoPro, and I had a strong feeling that a nature-inspired approach could be used to address the imbalance at the core of the tech industry too.

I saw a post on the Biomimicry Institute's Instagram

about "Nature's 10 Unifying Patterns," which are "the 10 most essential lessons from the natural world that should be considered as part of a design process."[4] This seemed like the perfect starting point for a "gap analysis," which we often did at work. A gap analysis compares the current state of an organization with its desired state and provides a plan for closing the identified gaps. In this case, I was going to compare the tech industry's dynamics with those of nature and visualize how the gaps might be closed. This is a summary of the comparison.

Comparing Nature's 10 Unifying Patterns[5] to the Tech Industry's Patterns (2017)

1. Optimizing versus Maximizing
While nature optimizes rather than maximizes, tech maximizes profit at the expense of others instead of optimizing for a balance of profit and collective well-being.

2. Objective versus Subjective
While nature runs on objective information, tech's data reflect the biases in the world, especially those of its data teams and decision-makers. For example, only 18 percent of data science employees in the United States and 11 percent of tech executives are female,[6] so data is collected and applied from a predominantly masculine perspective.

3. Recycling versus Discarding
While nature recycles all materials, tech discards and replaces employees rather than retraining or repurposing them to meet evolving needs.

4. Cooperation versus Competition

While nature rewards cooperation, tech rewards competition as it continuously evaluates the performance of employees against peers to determine who to reward and who to discard.

5. Safe versus Unsafe

While nature uses materials that are safe for living beings, tech uses a combination of safe and unsafe materials for living beings. Tech blends information from verified and unverified sources and develops undisclosed algorithms that can negatively impact consumers.

6. Local versus Global

While nature is locally attuned and indiscriminately responsive, tech is globally attuned and selectively responsive. Tech responds rapidly to global circumstances impacting profit, but is slow to address concerns about consumer and employee health and local gentrification.

7. Responsive versus Reactive

While nature is resilient to disturbances, tech is reactive to disturbances. Tech addresses disturbances with quick fixes rather than processing, healing, and adjusting.

8. Creativity versus Conformity

While nature uses shape to determine function, tech uses function to determine shape. Tech uses narrow, inflexible job descriptions and expects job seekers to conform rather than creating roles for talented candidates who could elevate tech products with their unique gifts and perspective.

9. Abundant resources versus Limited resources

While nature builds using abundant resources, tech builds using limited resources. Tech creates self-imposed limits on human resources via its narrow hiring criteria and discarding of existing employees, contributing to the shortage of approximately three million "qualified" tech and science workers in the United States.[7]

10. Moderate energy versus Excess energy

While nature uses only the energy it needs, tech uses excess energy as it wastes time, money, and potential by aligning with its biases instead of nature's unifying patterns.

I was impressed by how concisely and thoroughly this exercise captured the pain points I had experienced in the tech industry. I'd been dealing with them as they emerged over the course of a decade, but this was the first time I saw all the broken pieces assembled, like a stained-glass mosaic. The next step was to shine a light of hope through for myself.

The big question was whether anything could be done to close the gaps between nature and tech?

In an ideal world, tech employers would address the biases they had been made aware of, such as sexism, ageism, and racism. They would take account of collective well-being when making decisions. Employees would have organized advocacy, with better job security and a greater voice in shaping corporate culture and products. Hiring criteria would be broader and more flexible. Consumer experiences would be more transparent, safe, and inclusive.

In the real world, however, I was doubtful that tech employers would proceed differently unless they were legally obliged. Employees weren't likely to speak up for themselves or experiment with ideas that could benefit the company because their livelihoods were at stake. Consumers didn't have guidelines or sufficient information to make healthy choices online. What seemed most plausible for addressing the gaps between nature and tech was for consumers, consumer advocates, researchers, the government, and others outside of the industry to bring about change collectively. This had worked in the food and tobacco industries.

Standard nutrition labels were added to food products in the U.S. in response to consumer demand and evolved as research uncovered more about the relationship between diet and disease. Eliminating artificial trans fats from the U.S. food supply was accomplished via "a strategic combination of research, advocacy, corporate campaigns, communications, grassroots mobilization, legislation, regulatory actions, and litigation against companies and government."[8] After research revealed the health risks of smoking cigarettes and breathing secondhand smoke, smoking became less socially acceptable and increasingly restrictive legislation was passed to discourage cigarette use and reduce involuntary exposure. Each of these achievements unfolded over the course of decades.

The tech industry had parallels to these examples, providing a good starting point for the questions to ask. For example:

- Could guidelines be established for recommended daily online intake?

- Should online products be required to display the list of "ingredients" in their algorithms?
- Were there any harmful ingredients that needed to be eliminated from online products (e.g., disinformation or "black box" algorithms that lacked transparency even to their creators)?
- Were there health issues linked to excessive online product consumption (e.g., technology addiction or depression)?
- Were there health issues linked to secondhand exposure of online product consumption (e.g., secondhand depression)?

Since answering these questions and addressing them with legislation could take many years, I imagined what consumers could do in the meantime.

I had recently started hearing more about intuitive eating and learned that it helped to prevent eating disorders. According to the National Eating Disorders Association, "intuitive eating is about trusting your inner body wisdom to make choices around food that feel good in your body, without judgment and without influence from diet culture ... Intuitive eating is a beautiful part of recovery. It is also an essential piece in the prevention of eating disorders."[9] I believed that if consumers developed the ability to listen to their bodies' inner wisdom, this could also be helpful in avoiding unhealthy online choices too.

For five years I had been using my intuition to navigate the online world with positive results. When I started using this method at Yahoo!, it was difficult to sustain, but over time it became second nature. Actually, it was more like a reclaiming of my "first nature." I came to think of intuition as nature's algorithm that prioritizes personal health rather than corporate profits.

This isn't to say that every single one of my online choices was healthy and satisfying. I did occasionally lapse into unconscious online activity, the same way I occasionally lapsed into emotional eating, but overall my choices enhanced the quality of my life and brought me joy. For example, the top two apps I used on my iPhone were Pokemon GO and Google Maps. Pokemon GO got me outside walking and making new friends locally, which was something I had been struggling with. Google Maps' offline feature helped me navigate remote areas in the redwoods with no cell service, such as the place I did my daily sit spot.

I periodically reviewed my activity online to see how it felt in my body and to develop an awareness for any general patterns. For example, I looked at my Google Search history on myactivity.google.com and observed that I had been doing a couple of hundred searches a day on topics like starting a business, designing a website, and exploring new places. This felt light and tingly in my stomach. However, I also noticed that I had been doing "clusters" of searches in the middle of the night about twice a week, looking for answers on how to deal with people who stressed me out. I had a habit of rephrasing these searches multiple times, as though the right combination would unlock a magic solution. This felt heavy and tight in my stomach.

Reviewing personal activity data seemed like a quick and convenient way for consumers to get a feel for "intuitive online consumption," but I realized that many consumers might not want to experiment with using their intuition. I imagined that if an inside-out approach wasn't appealing, perhaps an outside-in approach would be. I came up with the notion that developing in-person friendships with emotionally healthy people could lead to healthier online choices because decisions would be made *from* a place of fulfillment rather than *to* find fulfillment. This would be another low-risk option for aligning more with nature's dynamics and surrendering less to technology's dynamics.

For five years I had been following the guidance I received from my redwood tree to seek out and connect with people who were wise, mature, and resilient. I gradually befriended a handful of women in their sixties, seventies, and eighties who were thriving, radiant, and had solid friendships in their lives. Spending time with them naturally curbed my desire to be on social media because of the quality and depth of the connections. There was a level of safety and trust that simply wasn't available online. I wished that wise, mature, resilient women had a voice within tech companies and in the healing process for the industry.

I pictured the stained-glass mosaic of the broken pieces of the tech industry again, and now I could see rays of hope shining through. It felt possible for positive shifts in the tech industry to occur. I envisioned that, in the long-term, using data as a creative tool would be taught as a core competency in school, like writing. There would also be data artisans who would share "recipes" for how to use data to create beautiful things, bring people together, and help the planet. Consumers would modify the recipes to their tastes and begin developing their own recipes as they became more proficient.

I felt ready to roll up my sleeves and get to work. My short-term goal was to identify a starting point for Data for Joy, gather information, and then reassess. I talked with people inside and outside the industry and listened for how I could best be of service. I also worked with a coach, who sent me into nature to listen for further insights and then helped me interpret and organize the information.

I would try to empower tech employees with the tools and resources to have longer, more fulfilling careers. I wanted to work with employers to increase employee retention and satisfaction, especially for women. This had the potential to improve productivity and profits for employers while bringing more balance to the industry and its products. My coach and I sketched out my next steps, and she also recommended a one-week nature-connection camp that she thought would resonate with me because I had mentioned wanting more training in this area.

The camp happened to start the day after the coach sent me the website link, and I couldn't get in touch with anyone to see if there was space or what to bring or expect. My intuition told me to pack some camping gear and just show up, even though it was a four-hour drive to get there. It turned out to be amazing.

The camp mimicked a village, and there were hundreds of participants. I was pleasantly surprised to see a mix of ages and genders. Every age range was celebrated, from babies to eighties, and organizers freely talked about menstrual cycles and menopause in mixed company, which felt shocking at first and then liberating. There was a council of elders and a rite of passage ceremony for teens. When a participant in their early twenties came to me for my experience, I was thrown off because that rarely happened in the tech industry. It was glorious to spend a week in an environment that treated aging as a normal part of life instead of an unacceptable, grim fate.

When I returned home, I felt energized and creative. I designed a program to help tech workers navigate their careers by using their intuition, examining their personal data, and aligning with nature's unifying patterns. I created a website describing my experience in the tech industry and offering the program, which I called Tech Support. If I gave hope to even one burnt-out tech employee by assuring them they weren't alone, it would be worth the effort.

I reached out to some employers, but the few which responded weren't open to hearing ideas for improving employee retention and satisfaction, despite the potential benefits to their bottom line. Employees I spoke with acknowledged the problems of the tech industry, but most felt like nothing could be done and had just accepted the situation. A few people thanked me for exploring ways to create change and asked how they could support me, but I didn't know what to ask for yet. A few others said I shouldn't waste my energy and offered to help me get a job in their organizations. Not one person I spoke with said they loved their job. All of this was helpful information.

I knew there must be other people out there trying to work toward the same goals I had. I wrote to like-minded organizations that I found online but didn't receive any responses.

I found that people outside of the tech industry were more open to experimenting with ways to improve their careers and lives, so I worked with them and had some successes. Then I went back into the tech setting to do a few presentations based on what I had learned. The presentations were positively received, elicited good discussions, and resulted in clients.

I also got my first "hater." A woman wrote to me multiple times after seeing my website to tell me I was an embarrassment and should stick to my looks. What immediately popped into my head, oddly, was the Heimlich maneuver (the well-known first aid procedure to assist someone who is choking, consisting of abdominal thrusts). I didn't know why that came up, so I googled it and discovered that it had been invented in 1974, when "choking on food or foreign objects like toys was the sixth-leading cause of accidental death in America."[10] I had assumed that the procedure had been around long before I was born. I imagined that in 1974, in a restaurant somewhere, a person choked and a patron who had just learned about the Heimlich maneuver had to decide whether to use it. They might look foolish to other patrons who hadn't heard of the procedure or even appear to be assaulting the choking victim, creating panic. Given that the alternatives included cutting the person's trachea open or standing by and watching them die, the temporary embarrassment was clearly worth it.

What I took from this was that Data for Joy may have looked crazy to some people, but I knew I couldn't stand by and do nothing. I had heard that someone on GoPro's new data team suffered a heart attack, which for me validated the need for some type of help. I decided to think of Data for Joy as avant-garde rather than embarrassing and continued onward.

After my initial wave of clients, I found it challenging to find new one, which was a common problem for new coaches. The general guidance in coaching programs was to leverage one's network for leads. As an introverted female in a male-dominated field, I didn't have much of a network so I decided to try advertising on Facebook and Twitter. At first it felt contradictory to advertise on the very platforms I felt were major contributors to the imbalance in the online world, but then it seemed fitting to inject these platforms with healing content. Unfortunately, it didn't work, so I stopped advertising.

Just when I was wondering what to try next, a lovely friend I had made at the week-long village invited me to a two-day event for female entrepreneurs that focused on sales and marketing. She had invited me to several workshops held in the redwoods that helped me walk the fine line between holding a starry-eyed vision while being grounded enough to take practical steps forward. The female entrepreneurs event would be our first time in a commercial setting, and I wasn't sure what to expect.

The event, held in an auditorium, received newspaper coverage. Several hundred women were in attendance and the onstage activities were glamorous and entertaining, like a Las Vegas show. The organizer shared her philosophy and path to success, led activities to help audience members connect with each other, and then brought out scores of perfect-looking, highly-accomplished women who had created profitable businesses through a program she offered. Afterwards, the women on stage came down to mingle with audience members and answer questions.

One of the women approached me and talked to me about my business like we were old friends. Admittedly, it was nice to have someone who could relate to the challenges I was facing and had overcome them, but I didn't know what to make of it all. Was this a charm school? A pyramid scheme? A cult? Legitimate? After the mingling session, we were told to digest the events of the day and sleep on it. Then, in the morning, if we wanted to sign up for the program we would get a substantial discount. A deposit would be required, which was fully refundable if we changed our minds within a few days.

When I went to sleep that night, I wasn't considering signing up for the program. In the morning, however, I meditated and got the feeling I should sign up, which was unexpected. I didn't look or act like the women on the stage, but I definitely needed help with my sales and marketing skills. I figured it wouldn't hurt to sign up, mull it over for a few days, and ask for my deposit back if I determined the program wasn't right for me. The organizer struck me as an honest person who would return the deposit without issues. My friend knew her personally and decided to sign up for the program too.

The second day of the event included outdoor activities which were tastefully executed. The grand finale, however, didn't sit well with me. In the final minutes, the audience was showered with fake dollar bills thrown from the balconies while upbeat music played and the women on stage clapped and cheered. In that moment I realized two things. One was how much I missed having a steady paycheck, and the other was that I didn't want to be in a program that used tactics like this. I didn't say anything to my friend, however, because she looked energized by the experience and had scooped up some of the bills to put on her vision board.

My friend and I described the event, including the grand finale, to the couple she worked for. We told them about the special discount we were offered for signing up during the event and asked what they thought. The husband responded in a deadpan voice, "Did they include a ShamWow with that?" I laughed hard. It was the reality check I needed, and I was glad to be with people who had our best interests at heart.

The next morning I requested a refund of my deposit. Within an hour I received a phone call from one of the women on stage who had shared her business success story. Her tone was quite different now. She twisted the popular coaching tagline "invest in yourself" and told me that if I didn't invest in their particular program I must not value myself. I replied that I did value myself and I didn't want to be in their program and that both could be true. We went back and forth multiple times, with each of us standing our ground. Then she said that my business would probably fail if I dropped out. She mentioned that she had tried to get her business going for several years and this was the only program that had worked for her. I asked if there was a money-back guarantee, and she said no. I asked for some specifics about the program, but the answers I received were vague. After forty minutes of trying to convince me to stay in the program, the woman sounded exasperated. She said she would issue my refund immediately and asked if I would be willing to talk more the next day. I said yes because I wondered what she would say, but she never called back. I received my refund promptly.

I was glad I experienced these bullying and fear-based sales tactics firsthand. It brought up the mixed feelings I had about the coaching industry, which was unregulated. Coaching provided a much needed space for women to experiment with creating profitable, feminine-based businesses. Unfortunately, the experimental nature meant that consumers needed to proceed with caution, not unlike the tech industry. For example, some coaching business models included selling client email addresses, resulting in a barrage of spam. On the positive side, when coaching was done well it could be life-changing. I had huge breakthroughs in a handful of programs, which more than made up for the negative experiences along the way.

At the time, I was a few months into an excellent online program that helped women create conscious businesses and projects. While I didn't have any existential epiphanies, the course helped me shift direction without feeling attached to my original plans. I noticed there were a number of participants developing projects that benefited the world but didn't generate income. I was reminded that the Heimlich maneuver saved people's lives but didn't generate income either. I realized that I was trying to fit Data for Joy into a business model that wasn't right for it. It occurred to me that it might be better suited as a research project, but I didn't have adequate funding. The voice in my head telling me I needed a regular paycheck was becoming louder and more persistent. I knew it would be time to return to the workforce soon.

A couple of weeks later, my intuition told me to go to the

online program's Facebook group. I came across a post from a woman offering complimentary financial services to fellow participants on a first-come, first-serve basis. I felt the need to reply to this generous offer, even though I didn't have any specific financial questions. I didn't realize it at the time, but this woman was going to become my long-term mentor and things were about to unfold in my life such that we wouldn't get to the topic of finances for a few years!

Shortly after I met my mentor, my life abruptly caved in. My significant other disappeared with a single phone call "to work on [himself]," whatever that meant. We had had a wonderful relationship, so I felt blindsided. Next, after fifteen years, my best friend disappeared from my life without saying goodbye due to an ultimatum from his new girlfriend, who had never met me. The ultimatum included having to evict his ex-girlfriend who was renting out his basement suite. He initially told me that he didn't want to set the precedent of taking orders, but the next thing I knew he had handed his life over and was posting happy relationship photos on social media. I couldn't believe this was the same free spirit who attended the 1969 People's Park protest by himself when he was seven years old and roamed from one national park to the next as a rock climbing guide for years. In one fell swoop, I lost the two people closest to me, and I felt a tremendous sense of abandonment and betrayal. In the midst of all this, a person I loved died.

My weekly calls with my mentor revolved around these losses, and she shared a variety of tools to help me through this period. I also met with the coaching partner from the program I completed after leaving GoPro, and her ability to hold space for me was highly comforting. I began doing a sit spot at the beach for an hour at the same time I used to talk to my significant other in the evenings. My friend from the week-long village invited me to attend a workshop that addressed healing from trauma. I started somatic therapy, which is "a form of body-centered therapy that looks at the connection of mind and body."[11] The therapist suggested I "talk" to the knots in my stomach to receive guidance from them. I realized that I had a lot of people helping me through this challenging time, and I had come a long way since my burnout at GoPro in terms of support and recovery.

Every day I wrote down a list of things that made me grateful, which is a practice widely recommended for coping with grief and trauma. Even though I continued to feel immense sadness, I could see I was making progress in my healing, which instilled me with a sense of hope. One of the items that always appeared on my list was my housing situation. My apartment was the nicest place I had ever lived, and the ocean setting near the redwoods was idyllic. Perhaps the best part was that I had lived there for more than seven years and the landlord had never raised the rent! In a normal housing market this would be remarkable, but in the midst of a severe housing crisis it was nothing short of miraculous. Nearby apartment complexes had more than doubled the rents. If my landlord had done the same, leaving GoPro and creating Data for Joy wouldn't have been possible.

Unfortunately, there was an echo chamber of negativity toward my landlord in the apartment complex. My "black hole" neighbor had consistently complained about him since the day I moved in, claiming he did "nothing," even though an abundance of evidence proved the contrary. Other tenants began repeating her gripes until it became the most popular conversation topic. One minute we would be talking about the weather and the next someone would begin moaning about how the landlord did nothing. When I interjected positive things about the landlord, I was met with silence.

One day, when I heard my neighbor complaining about the landlord for the umpteenth time, I pictured muting her with a remote control in my hand. I tried focusing on the sound of the waves crashing in the distance. For a moment, it helped. I was reminded that negativity tends to be noisier in intensity and frequency than peace and to weigh them accordingly in my thinking. In the music industry, mixing engineers adjust the volume levels of different tracks to achieve a balanced sound in a song. In the data industry, analysts rescale variables, such as age and income, to comparable ranges so they receive equal consideration in analyses. I needed to lower the volume of my chronically negative neighbor and raise the volume on my daily gratitudes to heal more quickly.

As I started to feel better in my personal life, I saw a news story about a homeless web developer in Silicon Valley who stood in the street wearing interview clothes and holding up a sign that read, "HUNGRY 4 SUCCESS. TAKE A RESUME." He had come to Silicon Valley from Texas to create his own tech startup but had run out of cash. He was applying for jobs but wasn't receiving callbacks. After the vehicle he was living in was repossessed, he resorted to sleeping on a park bench three miles from Google's headquarters. His story went viral on social media, and he was suddenly flooded with calls from tech employers, including Google.[12] I realized that if an entrepreneurial young male with a technical degree and work experience ended up homeless in a favorable job market, I could be next.

While creating Data for Joy, I spent most of my savings. I had no regrets. Several tech employees reached out to me and expressed appreciation for having someone to talk to because their friends, family, and those outside of the industry often didn't understand how unhealthy the culture was and dismissed their concerns. I was exposed to many new ideas, met amazing people, and experimented with my own way forward in a world that seemed to be changing faster than ever. I gained invaluable experience starting a business and trying to create change in the world. I followed my intuition and felt more confident doing so. I went for a routine physical examination and every single measurement was in the normal range. I felt at peace. It was time for me to return to the tech industry to apply what I had learned.

I started my job search by gathering data about myself, the job market, and relevant world events that might affect my search. Then, I analyzed the data and took action. As I received feedback from employers, I adjusted my actions. All of this was done playfully and quickly so that the process remained fun. I treated it like trying to find a romantic match: there needed to be compatibility and chemistry or it wasn't going to work out in the long-term. The following pages illustrate the 4 job search steps I followed.

When I received my first job offer, my intuition told me not to take it, and I listened. About a month later, I accepted a job offer I was genuinely excited about and was told I was the fastest hire they had ever made. I had applied to a total of thirty-one organizations, compared with more than 100 during my previous job search.

My new job was on the data team at a tech startup that served the restaurant industry, including seventeen of the top 100 restaurant chains in America. With all the food and eating analogies I used about data-driven products over the years, it felt like a fitting next chapter toward experimenting with using data for joy.

Step 1. Collect data

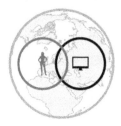

I spent half an hour jotting down my skills, interests, experience, causes, values, deal-breakers, and what my ideal job would look like (e.g., a three-day workweek.) I spent an hour researching the job market and perusing listings on hiring boards and websites of organizations I wanted to work for. I spent fifteen minutes reflecting on #metoo, the political divide, and other cultural shifts in the world. I also noted that California had added a new labor code banning employers from asking applicants for salary history.

Step 2. Analyze data

I tried to strike a balance between who I was, what I wanted in my ideal job, what openings were available, the cultural shifts in the world, and nature's unifying patterns. Then, I updated my résumé accordingly. I re-read the openings that most resonated with me, checked how well my résumé answered their call, and tweaked it further.

Step 3. Take action

I applied for jobs sourced from hiring boards, company websites, my network, and organizations which contacted me. I also sent proposals to a few employers who didn't have relevant openings. These led to phone screenings, in-person interviews, and offers.

Step 4. Repeat

As I received the results from my first batch of applications, I analyzed them with my mentor. We celebrated each step I completed in the hiring "funnel" and came up with action items from lessons learned, such as modifying the criteria I used to decide which jobs to apply for. We repeated this cycle as more results came in.

Figures 2 to 5 illustrate the job search steps I followed

CHAPTER 5
TRANSFORMATION

I eagerly anticipated my first day at the startup. I missed working with big data and, even more so, I missed being part of a team.

The startup helped restaurants find technology solutions for issues such as online ordering. The main offering was a loyalty and engagement platform, which included end-to-end support for loyalty programs and campaigns. Analytics were integral to quantifying outcomes and providing insights into consumer activity.

What I liked most about the startup's business model was that there were no "gotchas" for consumers, who proactively provided their email address (referred to in the industry as zero-party data) in return for rewards and special offers. The startup provided analytics on consumer orders and loyalty program activity (referred to as first-party data) to help the restaurants better serve and retain them. There was no third-party advertising or selling of personal information. It was a mutually beneficial, trustworthy relationship between the startup, its customers (restaurants), and their customers (consumers). The industry was trending towards zero- and first-party data business models thanks to the General Data Protection Regulation passed by the European Union and the California Consumer Privacy Act, both of which came into effect in 2018.

I was hired to create a bucket testing team in the startup's Silicon Valley headquarters, but by the time I joined the company its needs had changed. I was to be the only business intelligence (BI) employee based in the United States while the other seven people on the team were in Jaipur, India. The Jaipur team included a few employees who had been with the startup for several years and were highly knowledgeable about its data and systems. While I was concerned about working in isolation, I felt lucky to have access to the data experts and hoped to ramp up as quickly as possible.

I began planning a trip to the Jaipur office to receive training. My boss, who was the head of the data team, encouraged me to time my trip such that I could attend the wedding of the head of the BI team. She had invited the entire startup of 300 employees to her wedding! I was thrilled!

My boss filled me in on the logistics of booking the trip, which required things like ordering business cards and picking a religion from the list on the business visa application (being non-religious wasn't one of the choices.) The human resources (HR) department helped me with booking lodging and transportation. The interim head of the BI team took it upon himself to be in touch with me during every leg of my twenty-two-hour trip until I arrived safely. He told me before my trip that the state of Rajasthan was known for its hospitality and that they were even hospitable to their enemies! I could feel the hospitality from halfway around the world and knew this was going to be a special trip.

My adventure began with a sixteen-hour flight to Delhi.

Domestic flights in the United States are strict about passengers staying in their seats with their seatbelts on, but on my flight most passengers left their seats as soon as the plane reached cruising altitude, and they continued to socialize in the aisles for the rest of the flight. I found myself chitchatting with strangers, who offered a lot of advice about what to see and where to go during my visit. Word got out that it was my first trip to India, and the flight attendants invited me to the back of the plane for a lassi and more advice.

My hotel in Jaipur was gorgeous, and I was treated like royalty. The staff frequently left gifts, cake, origami towel art, and personal messages in my room. Every morning one of the chefs made custom dishes for me that were absolutely scrumptious. Before work I would walk to the park nearby, which was bustling with groups of people exercising together. There was boot camp, walking, jogging, yoga, and so on. Several lovely people invited me to exercise with their groups. I couldn't believe all of this was real! It surpassed anything I had ever imagined.

The office was vibrant and buzzing with energy. On my first day, a section of the wall was transformed into a gratitude board and we left notes about what we appreciated about the people around us. It was the perfect way to start getting to know my co-workers. Unlike the employees in the United States, those in the Jaipur office were not supplied with monitors. At first I thought this was a bad thing, but then I realized that by not inserting large screens between everyone, we could see and talk to each other. It was the most connected corporate environment I had ever been in! Throughout my visit, each person on the team generously shared their knowledge with me and took me to different tourist sites. We ate lunch together daily, and one of my co-workers serenaded us on the roof of the office building afterwards.

Being in the office felt more like a vacation than a job, yet the team was highly productive. Each person specialized in a different area of the data, and while working on customers' requests they helped each other with the nuances and caveats. They often had to seek further clarification from other teams in the office, such as engineering and product management. I realized that no matter how much I learned during my trip, I would still need to contact the team quite often in order to work on requests too. Depending on this worried me, but I decided to go with the flow.

The head of HR in the Silicon Valley office checked in with me every day to make sure my stay was going smoothly and to see if I needed anything. I deeply appreciated that my safety and health were a high priority and had never received such attention from any HR department in my career. After a few days, I told her that she didn't need to call anymore because I was having the time of my life!

The weekend-long wedding was coming up, and I was excited. Multiple co-workers helped me shop for outfits and jewelry. The bride's mother also gifted me a stunning red sari as my outfit for one of the events and arranged to have my makeup done. I had no words to express what it felt like to be treated in this way. I felt joy radiating from my entire being.

The wedding weekend was dazzlingly colorful and festive. The bride, groom, and their families were regal and gracious. There was a freedom to proceedings that I hadn't experienced in western weddings. There was no RSVP, no gift giving, no assigned seating, and no preselected meal. The opportunities for drama and control had been virtually eliminated. My co-workers told me that if I was nicely dressed I could drop by other weddings I encountered without knowing anyone there. I was astonished. In the United States, one might be arrested for trespassing.

Toward the end of my visit, I went sightseeing to a palace. My soulful guide brought me to the original palace ruins behind it, which had become the village square. When we showed up, locals of all ages were playing cricket. There was a remarkable young girl who was one of the star players. Watching the match reminded me of the week-long village I attended, except that this was the real thing, centuries old and steeped in history. Witnessing this friendly community game among the ancient ruins made me feel alive and hopeful.

Next, the guide brought me to a temple where an ascetic was in prayer. Out front were some animals relaxing peacefully in the shade. Off to the left, some men were speaking in sweet tones about the lake that used to be there twenty years earlier. The ascetic, animals, and locals were each doing their thing in harmony, and I suddenly felt connected to absolutely everything. I wasn't sure what exactly happened, but I felt high, similar to the energetic experience I had with my redwood tree several years earlier. I could practically feel the stars while simultaneously being suspended in tranquility. With the redwood tree I felt timelessness, and here I felt "spaceless-ness." I was weightlessly present in a beautiful, simple, coexistence of everything. Many westerners describe these types of experiences in India. I didn't want to leave this spot, but it was time to go back to the hotel. I later returned to the village to hike and play games with some of the locals, who felt like old friends.

I was grateful that most of the startup's employees were located in this magical pink place on the opposite side of the planet from Silicon Valley (much of the old city of Jaipur is painted pink because it symbolizes hospitality). The generosity of my co-workers and everyone I encountered was so over-whelming that I didn't know how to handle it or reciprocate. This was the complete opposite of my life in Silicon Valley, and it felt surreal. Upon my departure, the team gifted me a framed photo collage of my adventures, which I continue to treasure.

Unfortunately, about four months into my job, the company culture in the Silicon Valley office began to shift and morale began to decline. One day, a woman who sat next to me asked for some figures for a meeting with a customer. When I looked for her a couple of hours later, I couldn't find her. I never saw her again. I began noticing other employees disappearing too. At the lunch table, the tone had become more serious and people began eating at their desks. I wondered if the startup was having problems.

During my next trip to India, I noticed that this shift had affected the Jaipur office too: the BI team was quieter and tended not to sit at the team table as much. The trip was still pleasant, and I was touched that the team waited for my arrival to do an offsite at Pushkar, a scenic and holy city in Rajasthan famous for its annual camel fair. I was quiet too because I was exhausted. The effects of working in opposite time zones were catching up to me. During daylight saving time, Jaipur was 12.5 hours ahead of California and during standard time it was 13.5 hours ahead. This meant inter-office meetings often occurred at odd hours and that traveling between offices came with maximum jet lag. I was feeling off-kilter almost all the time.

A couple of weeks before my third trip to India, someone in my management chain asked why I was traveling so much and raised their voice at me. I was puzzled because when I joined the startup the same person told me that I was required to travel to India once a quarter. This was my third quarter on the job and I was doing my third trip to India. It turned out that new travel budgets had been created but not communicated. I ended up canceling my trip and decided not to travel again unless I was asked to do so in writing. Eventually, I was told that the data team could only travel between offices once a year. I thought this policy was short-sighted and would lead to delays and miscommunications with internal and external customers.

Right before the change in travel policy, I submitted a blog for the company website about best practices for collaborating across time zones. Spending time face to face with colleagues was one of the main recommendations I offered, as not everything could be documented. My blog hadn't been published yet and, in light of the tension around the topic of travel, I asked for it not to be. I was reported to the HR department, and it was my moment of realization that the startup was going through the same type of bipolarity I had experienced at Yahoo! and GoPro. I was asked to write another blog post. I tried several times but couldn't. I never would have applied for the job had I known I could only see once a year the team I relied on to get my basic daily tasks done. In my opinion, that was a recipe for failure for everyone involved.

Soon afterwards my team was told to start being frenemies with other employees in the hope of improving productivity and accountability. I had a flashback to the dysfunctionality at Yahoo! and braced myself. At a couple of meetings I was told to be more like one of the other employees. "I love that guy! I want to buy a house for him! You should try to be more like him!" I found it interesting that the person I was told to emulate engaged in "subtle bullying" behaviors such as ignoring, excluding, minimizing, undermining, and taking credit for the work of others.

I was given a new responsibility of staffing the data help chat every weekday afternoon Pacific Time. The data help chat consisted of real-time questions and urgent requests from the customer success team in Texas. The team in Jaipur rotated to cover the morning hours. I was expected to acknowledge new chats within fifteen minutes, which meant that I was frequently disrupted when trying to focus on bigger tasks.

One day, an urgent request came through for one of our biggest customers, whose reports employed custom logic and were built by someone in Jaipur. I wasn't familiar with the details of the logic, so I couldn't solve the urgent request. I was berated and told that I needed to know the logic of every single report. There were more than 100 live customers and scores more in the pipeline. Each customer was provided with thousands of data points with variations in logic and interpretation, depending on their setup and preferences. It was unrealistic to expect anyone to learn the variations of all figures in all the reports, especially through messaging and Zoom calls at odd hours.

A few days later, the CEO took a couple of teams to lunch and told us that the office environment might seem quite stressful at the moment but it was part of a growth phase. He said that a few years earlier the company experienced a similar transition that lasted several months. He asked us to hang tight, assuring us the situation would get better. Then he invited questions and answered them all. I appreciated his proactive approach and accessibility, but I wasn't convinced that the challenges I was facing at work would improve any time soon.

I decided to start casually looking for another job and encountered a new twist in undesirable Silicon Valley labor practices when researching the employment market. I read that a majority of Google's workforce was made up of temps and contract workers who were "underpaid and overworked" compared with the full-time employee minority.[1] The twist was that these workers were technically employees of outside agencies so they were not included in Google's employee metrics such as median salary and tenure. One Google employee described the experience of temps and contractors as a "white-collar sweatshop."[2] I was tremendously disappointed that Google chose to have a "shadow workforce" because they were normalizing the practice for the rest of the industry. With annual profits of more than $30 billion, it seemed especially scandalous to underpay workers and sweep the statistics under the carpet.

I found myself feeling more frustrated than ever with Silicon Valley. The leaders of the largest tech companies were older and more experienced now, and I had hoped their choices would become wiser and less harmful to others. It seemed to be the opposite. I no longer wanted to live or work in the area, but I didn't know where to go. I decided to keep an open mind and see where I felt most drawn to.

In October 2019, I received a flash of clarity.

The utility company in my area, Pacific Gas and Electric (PG&E), decided to shut off the power to more than two million people as a pre-emptive measure to prevent wildfires. PG&E had caused scores of fires in the past, such as the 2018 Camp Fire, which was the "deadliest and most destructive fire in California history."[3] Decades of power infrastructure negligence combined with drier, windier weather patterns had led to this situation. Unfortunately, my apartment complex used an electric well pump, so power outages came with water outages too.

I decided to leave town and encountered a long line at the gas station, which had four pumps. One pump was monopolized by a person filling container after container with gas as though it were never going to be sold again. At another pump, I saw someone accidentally break the nozzle, rendering it unusable. This left only two pumps available to the growing line of cars. When my turn came, a car from the street swooped in and cut me off. The person appeared to be under the influence of something. I cautiously pointed out the line to them, but they proceeded to fill their tank and then not leave after they were done. This left only one pump for people who were waiting in line, which struck me as a metaphor for life in the area. Greed, disrepair, and substance abuse were unchecked and tied up resources. People who followed the rules had to fend for themselves using what slim pickings were left and were expected to do so with compassion and a smile.

I drove several hours away and stayed with friends. It was wonderful to leave the Silicon Valley bubble to remind myself that there were less extreme people and places in the world. On the drive home, an idea came to me of where to move. I recalled a peaceful ocean town in Oregon I had fallen in love with a decade earlier on a road trip. It was a remote place and I knew it was a longshot, but as soon as I got home I checked to see if there were any data jobs available there. I found a listing at a health organization that sounded perfect! I thanked my intuition for sending the listing my way and realized that the time away from Silicon Valley helped me connect with my inner guidance.

I ended up receiving a job offer from the health organization, and I was elated! During the interview process, the team was extremely welcoming and lively. One of the members who also used to work in Silicon Valley looked relaxed and happy in his new life. I quickly accepted the job offer and submitted my resignation to my boss.

That weekend, a personal issue arose that required traveling to the East Coast. For future reference, I looked up the travel time from the town in Oregon to my destination and saw that it would take as long as my trips to India! I started to have doubts about whether to move to a place so isolated from everyone I knew. I could feel how wonderful it would be to start over in a beautiful location with kind co-workers, but I began to feel torn. I talked to my mentor, meditated in nature, and was finally able to hear my intuition, which told me to stay where I was. This wasn't the answer I wanted to hear, and I was angry that my intuition had guided me to find the job in the first place. I had wasted the time of the team which hired me, and I wasn't sure I would be allowed to stay in the startup after resigning.

I considered overriding my intuition, but knew that I would probably regret it. After I decided to trust it, I immediately felt better. I knew that intuition is based on knowledge and that perhaps some new information came up that wasn't available when I applied for the job. The same dynamic happened routinely at work: decisions changed and evolved continuously based on new data. I took a deep breath and told myself that everything would be okay.

I had a difficult time telling the person who would have been my new boss that I had changed my mind about the job. He was gracious, which made it even harder to give up the chance to leave Silicon Valley for a promising new life. When I asked my current boss if I could keep my job, he said that he hadn't submitted my resignation letter because he knew I would stay. He had a certain boldness and confidence that made him a strong leader, and I was tremendously grateful for it that day.

Things at work improved immediately. A new person joined the data team and began assisting with the data help chat during afternoons. I started working on a couple of larger projects I was excited about. The first was a collaboration with my boss to speed up the top customer-facing dashboard while reducing costs. The second was to design the data processing for consumer order analytics. Nobody else on the team specialized in this area of the data, so I would be able to work relatively independently. I had pictured myself analyzing consumer consumption activity when I accepted the job at the startup, and now it was coming to fruition. I wondered if the act of resigning had played a role in shifting resources and opportunities towards me. By the end of the year, I felt like I had found my groove at work. It turned out that the CEO had been correct about things getting better.

When 2020 began, many people in the office were sick. The company all-hands was canceled twice in January due to multiple executives being severely ill. Someone who sat near me said that he had gotten so sick after returning from Asia that he thought he was going to die. At the time, we all assumed it was the flu, but in hindsight it might have been COVID.

In mid-January, the person who sat next to me told me that he thought COVID was going to become a widespread problem. He opened a map of China and showed me that Wuhan was a crossroads for major highways and waterways (the Yangtze and Han rivers). It was also the most populous city in central China and a hub for commerce and trading, ideal circumstances for spreading the virus. He predicted a global outbreak followed by a stock market crash, inflation, and then a period of creativity and innovation. He was one of the smartest people I had ever met and barely talked unless he had something important to say, so I listened attentively. A month later, I overheard a couple of executives dismiss COVID as "hype from worried soccer moms."

I found the disparity in the conversations about COVID fascinating. It reminded me that truth seems to come in whispers (I had to physically lean over and put my hand to my ear to hear the person next to me) while machismo seems to have a built-in megaphone. It's not truth's job to adjust its transmission to me. Rather, I need to have my internal receiver tuned to the appropriate frequency range.

On the last day of February, I was excited to go to an art studio in the redwoods for its annual collage workshop. I looked forward to spending a full day in the forest. For the center of my collage, I chose the photo of Michelle Obama on the cover of *AARP Magazine*'s October 2011 issue. There were thousands of magazines in the art studio to pick from, and I was intuitively drawn to it as soon as I walked in. Another image I put on my collage was of two monks laughing heartily. They were having more fun in the monastery than I was in my apartment complex, which made me laugh. When I got home, I hung up the collage so I could look at it every day.

A couple of weeks later, the COVID lockdown began. The startup immediately performed a round of layoffs due to widespread restaurant closures and uncertainty about the industry's path forward. Unfortunately, the person who assisted with the data help chat was among those laid off. He was talented and well-liked, but he was also the newest employee on the team, which was disadvantageous when it came to layoffs.

On the plus side, for the first time in my career I got to work from home full-time. Marissa Mayer's remote work ban at Yahoo! had become an industry standard that hadn't shown any signs of changing. It never occurred to me that it could flip to the opposite in an instant. I wished it hadn't taken a pandemic for it to do so, but it gave me hope that anything was possible when it came to transforming the tech industry.

Meanwhile, in my personal life a number of people in my orbit suddenly became paranoid. My significant other, who had no history of mental illness, was convinced he was being followed by Russian spies. He was trying to ferret out the potential double-agents among his friends, and he became overly talkative and religious too, giving away all his money. A couple of other people I knew were experiencing similar personality changes and delusions that others were out to get them.

My significant other went through a couple of psychiatric evaluations, and each time he was released the next day in exactly the same state he entered. I was told that he was in psychosis, a disorder in which a person loses touch with reality. It was my first time learning about psychosis and how the mental healthcare system handles these cases. It turns out that people in psychosis get to decide for themselves whether to seek treatment and, not surprisingly, they often choose not to because they believe their hallucinations and delusions to be real. It was a Catch-22: if someone thought they needed psychiatric treatment, it demonstrated they were of sound mind and didn't need any; and if they didn't think they needed psychiatric treatment, they were taken at their word and wouldn't receive any.

Friends and family had no option but to stand by and watch treatable conditions like this potentially escalate until the person physically harmed themselves or others. The system offered friends and families no support other than self-help videos and links to support groups run by others in the same situation.

I attended one support group meeting and listened to story after story about the toll of having a loved one experiencing a mental health crisis who was unwilling to receive treatment. One couple's adult child heard voices and drove his car into a brick wall, suffering major injuries and leaving his parents in emotional agony. The bright spot was that by injuring himself he was forced to receive mental health treatment. Another person's adult child became deeply paranoid and ended up moving back home after losing his job, housing, and friends. It broke the family apart. A woman's husband was in psychosis for the first time and said he planned to give their life savings to a church nearby, sending her into a major panic.

I was stunned that none of these family members were given professional support. I tried to find a therapist to help me navigate my own situation. The only local person I found charged several hundred dollars an hour, which I was not willing to pay.

I decided to try EAP since it had been a helpful resource for me when I was struggling with my job at GoPro. Just as before, EAP approved me for three free sessions with a therapist, but this time the wait was a month and the experience ended up being awful. I had a Zoom call with a therapist who listened for a while, told me it sounded like I was going through a lot, wished me luck in finding someone who could help me, and abruptly ended the call. I waited for them to reconnect, but they didn't. I had noticed the therapist looked disheveled and unfocused and wondered if they might have needed therapy themselves. Perhaps they were overwhelmed with the surge in demand for mental health services or were dealing with people with mental illness in their own lives. In any case, I didn't bother with the other two sessions and was frustrated that I had waited a month just to be hung up on. I was extremely grateful that I had my mentor, my coaching partner, and my friend from the week-long village to help me through this scary and uncertain situation. I'm not sure what I would have done without them.

Meanwhile, at work the pace was picking up and employees were told to work harder. Technology had become critical to restaurants' survival during the pandemic, which meant the startup was busier than ever. Data insights and reporting were in especially high demand as restaurants tried to understand the evolving dynamics of the channels used for placing and receiving orders as well as the changes in consumer consumption patterns. The work was interesting and meaningful, and I felt like I was in the right place at the right time for using data to help restaurants stay afloat during COVID. However, I was also starting to feel overwhelmed.

I was at home alone, glued to my laptop for so many hours a day on weekdays that I began developing queasiness and migraines. Combined with what I was dealing with in my personal life, I knew I wouldn't be able to keep up at work much longer. I talked to my boss, who suggested I take a leave of absence. This came as a huge relief to me, and I pictured myself healing quickly and being able to return to my projects soon.

As soon as I left work, I began spending time in nature and journaling, which reduced my headaches. I also contacted my health maintenance organization to see if it offered therapy, and it did. I was diagnosed with "adjustment disorder," also known as "situational depression," which is "a maladaptive response to a psychosocial stressor."[4] I qualified for individual and group therapy at minimal cost. I later read that during the first month of Poland's COVID quarantine, a survey showed a 49% increase in adjustment disorder symptoms,[5] and I wondered what the worldwide statistics were.

Group therapy changed my life. It was even better than the sharing circles at nature-connection gatherings because it went beyond holding space to healing and helping others. The moderator was a therapist and former caseworker who was brilliant at guiding group members to support each other and celebrate wins. I showed up to the first session feeling empty, struggling just to do the dishes. Within a few weeks, I had made noticeable progress and sharing my experience was useful to the newer members.

One member, who had been with the group for several

months, "graduated" shortly after I joined. He had worked through his issues, found an exciting job, and was relocating with his family to start a new chapter in his life. He made a slide presentation, with graphs, of his treatment journey, and it took my breath away. He had traversed the emotional spectrum from despair to joy with the support of a diverse group, in a trusted space led by a therapist, which operated on information. *This* was data for joy!

When my significant other finally started receiving treatment, I felt like I had shed a huge weight. I shared the news with my neighbors since they had seen his change in behavior, and they were wonderfully supportive. One woman invited me over and made me a delicious omelet. Another woman started a routine of going for walks with me a couple of times a week and didn't ask a single prying question, which I appreciated tremendously. Even my "black hole" complaining neighbor was extremely kind and understanding. I apologized to her for any problems my significant other might have caused, and she gave me a hug and reached out a couple of times afterwards to see how I was doing.

Throughout this time, I was thinking of author Ken Kesey. His 1962 novel, *One Flew Over the Cuckoo's Nest*, was the only impression I had of mental hospitals. Even though the novel was set in Oregon, it was based on Kesey's experience working in a Silicon Valley mental health facility. This led me to picture my significant other in similar circumstances and I felt quite anxious, even though I was relieved he was receiving treatment.

After writing the novel, Kesey moved to a log cabin in the redwoods, located near my special tree, where he hosted counterculture icons such as the Grateful Dead, the Hell's Angels, and Neal Cassady. I re-read Allen Ginsberg's 1965 poem, "First Party at Ken Kesey's with Hell's Angels," which described a rip-roaring party at the log cabin. That time felt long gone, especially with the pandemic lockdown.

Kesey's time in the log cabin ended after he served six months in prison in 1967 for marijuana possession. He began his prison sentence in the county jail and was later transferred to a minimum security prison in the redwoods, an honor camp, with no bars or gates, located near his cabin. There, the inmates cleared brush and participated in group therapy sessions. The idea seemed ahead of its time and one that would be useful for everyone, not just prisoners.

When I first moved to the coast, I hiked as close as I could to the former honor camp location because I was intrigued by Kesey's experience as well as the concept of rehabilitating prisoners in the redwoods with group therapy. The honor camp shut down in 2003 due to budget cuts, but it was such a nice location there were discussions of turning it into a public campground.

Now that I was in group therapy, I had even greater appreciation for the program at the redwood honor camp. I wished the space could be used to hold outdoor group therapy sessions for anyone struggling with the pandemic lockdown, which had turned everyone into prisoners of sorts. I tried hiking to the honor camp again, but the trail was in such disuse that I kept encountering giant spiderwebs and turned back. When my significant other was released from the hospital, I took him near the trailhead and he hugged a tree.

When it was my turn to graduate from group therapy, I was sad that it was over. The therapist recommended that I not mention participating in group therapy at my workplace because other patients had experienced negative outcomes when they did so. I heeded her advice because I knew there was stigma around anything relating to mental health. I wished the healthcare system addressed this issue. Why were annual physical exams standard practice but not annual mental exams? Why wasn't mental illness prevention as widely publicized as physical illness prevention?

When I returned to work, my manager and the HR department were extremely supportive. I told them that I wasn't back to my old self yet, and they gave me the option to return for three days a week for as long as I needed. I was touched by their generosity and cried with joy. I remembered that part of my ideal job description before joining the startup was having a three-day workweek, but it had felt unattainable. Now it was a reality. Though getting there involved significant personal trauma, I finally had the opportunity to work on a schedule that energized me.

The only downside to working part-time was, of course, lower pay. However, this felt like a minor sacrifice given all the positives. For one, I no longer felt off-kilter from working odd hours. In fact, I felt healthy and happy. This was the best work/life balance of my career, and the result was that I was getting as much done during a three-day workweek as I had during a five-day workweek! It was a win-win: my employer saved money while maintaining productivity, and I felt more alive and fulfilled.

Unfortunately, in August 2020 external events shook up day-to-day life again. An uncharacteristic lightning storm hit the area during which nearly 11,000 lightning flashes were recorded without any rain. It started hundreds of fires in California, including at the CZU Lightning Complex in the Santa Cruz Mountains and the Woodward Fire in Point Reyes National Seashore. High winds caused the CZU fire to spread rapidly through the redwood forest and gems like Big Basin Redwoods State Park suffered immense damage. The area of my special redwood tree was also affected, and it was closed indefinitely. I was heartbroken.

I flipped through a book of classic northern California hikes I had purchased nearly twenty years earlier and noticed that many of them no longer existed due to wildfires. I was glad I had done the hikes I was most interested in, but there were still a few that I planned to get to "someday." I assumed the hikes would be there when I was ready, but now I understood that anyone or anything could change in a flash, literally or figuratively. My workplace, personal life, and outdoor sanctuaries all changed radically in 2020.

A few weeks later, the greater San Francisco area awoke to "apocalyptic" skies—dark orange and sunless—caused by smoke from the multitude of fires. It felt like a day of reckoning for humanity's destructive relationship with nature and itself. Nobody could escape the sky's eeriness, no matter who they were or how much money they had. At least for one day, Silicon Valley leaders had to acknowledge a power higher than themselves.

On the local news, a reporter was interviewing passersby to get their impressions of the ominous skies. One woman said that she was on her way to get pizza because she needed comfort food. I automatically thought of work because many of our customers were pizza restaurants and some had been experiencing record sales in 2020. I had been asked to give a short data talk at the startup in a few weeks, and the primal vibe of the news clip inspired me to discuss data fundamentals and philosophy for decision-makers.

To prepare for the talk, I thought about Plato's cave, the ancient allegory in which prisoners are chained to a cave facing a blank wall. Behind them is a fire that casts shadows of objects onto the wall. To the prisoners, the shadows are their entire reality. If freed, the sunlight outside of the cave would hurt the prisoners' eyes, but eventually they would see actual objects instead of shadows and they would realize that their experience in the cave wasn't reality, after all. A modern-day version would be being held captive in a movie theater and believing the movies projected onto the screen were reality. With no outside information, the audience might not know that the content was fictional and scripted or that there were illusory special effects. The same idea held true for online screens. Projections of internet content might be perceived as reality until stepping outside into the sunlight. And the same idea held true with analytics in tech companies, even though the intent was for data to mimic reality as closely as possible. We all needed reality checks to keep things in perspective.

I sometimes encountered decision-makers who took the figures on reports as reality. When I pointed out discrepancies caused by factors such as data quality and availability issues, processing cost and speed constraints, and analysts' personal propensities, they seemed surprised. My talk was only going to be fifteen minutes' long, and I decided to illustrate some of the points using examples of questions I had encountered on the data help chat and in customer requests.

To begin, I defined the entities involved in restaurant loyalty programs as the consumer, the restaurant, and their contextual surroundings (e.g., competition from other local restaurants.) From these, the startup primarily collected data on restaurant transactions and campaign events because this was what was available and practical. This meant we gathered a lot of data on *what* consumers did (e.g., order pizza) but almost no data on *why* (e.g., they needed comfort food to cope with dark orange skies) and *how* it affected their lives afterwards (e.g., their anxiety was quelled but they got heartburn).

Restaurants routinely asked, "Why do loyalty customers stop coming back?" and it was a moment of truth about analytics. The potential reasons for a customer not returning were numerous and varied, such as moving away from the neighborhood, no longer enjoying the food, experiencing long wait times, not getting enough value from the loyalty program, rising car break-ins in the parking lot, or following the latest diet fad. Transaction data offered little insight. A few loyalty consumers wrote reviews that shed some light on potential areas of improvement for the restaurant and the loyalty app, but the ratings didn't have a strong correlation with whether consumers returned. Like any relationship in life, restaurants had to operate on incomplete and imperfect information when it came to building loyalty with consumers and could only control their own actions, such as running campaigns incentivizing consumers to return, acting on feedback in reviews, addressing staffing shortages, experimenting with new menu items, or modifying their loyalty program. Basically, there was educated guessing involved, and this was normal. All businesses had to operate on incomplete and imperfect information to varying degrees.

When it came to transaction data, it was used to compute success metrics such as the number of restaurant visits from loyalty consumers. Unfortunately, these figures didn't match reality perfectly for a variety of reasons. For example, if a loyalty consumer checked in at the restaurant, their visit could be identified. But what if the loyalty consumer forgot to check in? There were other types of loyalty transactions that could be used to identify their visit, such as redeeming a reward, but this calculation was costly and imprecise. Other than that, a loyalty consumer's visit could not be identified from the transaction data. Also, as part of consumer data privacy laws, loyalty consumers could request their data be removed from our platform, in which case their transaction data was deleted. The bottom line was that loyalty consumer visits were undercounted in analytics by an unknown amount.

Every data organization in every business encountered

similar gaps with reality. It was the bane of trying to project reality into numbers and then back into reality. Engineers used technology (e.g., a restaurant's point-of-sale system) to project a consumer's experience into transactions; data analysts projected these transactions into business success metrics, insights, and stories; and decision-makers projected these success metrics, insights, and stories into action items to help them achieve their business goals. It had the potential to be Plato's cave, cubed! Gaps with reality were to be expected, and stepping out into the sunlight would be a reminder not to equate analytics with reality.

To demonstrate how data analysts projected their own values and beliefs into their work, I came up with ideas on how to leverage data to help customers succeed based on my personal preferences. One of my ideas was to identify potential synergies between restaurants based on certain attributes and to help them help each other adjust their operations more quickly during COVID. I envisioned something like group therapy for restaurants, organized by the startup. My belief was that it wasn't only people who suffered from "adjustment disorder" but entities too. Data, like words, could be combined and applied in a subjective manner by analysts.

I sketched out the series of human projections in the end-to-end process of making data-driven decisions, with each projection offering the opportunity for personal values, biases, and mistakes to be infused, illustrated in Figure 6.

Figure 6. Human Projection in the Data-Driven Process

Given my talk was brief, I trimmed down my presentation and made it business-friendly. I received positive feedback from a few decision-makers in the startup, which led to some follow-up discussions. Until then, I didn't realize how much I needed to hear some praise. A number of my colleagues were still in frenemy mode, and my morale had been declining.

One colleague told me they were angry I got to work part-time and kept assigning me work on my days off even though I asked them multiple times to please stop. Another colleague hijacked the first twenty-three minutes of a presentation I was giving to management, even though I tried to regain control. Even more blatant, my name didn't appear on the list of BI team members in the startup's nominations for team of the year. The omission felt deliberate since the teams were generally self-nominated.

One particularly stressful day, a thought crossed my mind that it would be wonderful if I could join the big data team. I worked with them regularly without any issues. In fact, they were always kind and pleasant towards me. The head of the team was local and the rest of the team overlapped considerably with Pacific time zone business hours. I wasn't sure how to broach the topic with my manager, but I didn't have to. The next day, my manager offered me the opportunity to join the big data team! I was astonished and immediately accepted. I would get to keep my three-day workweek but still needed spend one day a week monitoring the data help chat and working on customer requests, leaving only two days a week to dedicate to the new team. I agreed.

After switching teams, someone from the previous team tried to micromanage a new project I was leading that didn't involve them and in which they had no expertise. My new boss sorted it out, and I finally started to feel free of the nonsense I had been dealing with. My productivity soared, and I loved my work. My new boss and I quickly cycled through projects, and he said that I got at least as much done as a full-time employee. I looked forward to Mondays again.

While things were going well for me, other employees in the company had reached their breaking points. One told me they were resigning because the work hours with India were unsustainable and impacted their family life too much. Another told me they were resigning because they had worked harder at the startup than anywhere else in their career and felt they were not rewarded for their efforts. Someone else told me they were looking for a new job because they were being treated badly. It turned out they were dealing with some of the same people who had been undermining me.

At the close of 2020, the data team held a hackathon over Christmas, which I had never encountered, even in Silicon Valley. Upper management loved the idea. I would have preferred to reflect together on the transformation of our workplace during 2020 and celebrate all we got done to support the restaurant industry during COVID. The startup's portfolio had grown to nearly 300 customers, including about thirty of the top 100 restaurant chains in America, and analytics became a critical tool for these customers to navigate the pandemic.

When 2021 started, I didn't know what to expect and I didn't try to guess.

One evening I was on a conference call with my friend from the week-long village, and she was going on about how she could manifest anything she wanted. She had just returned from a mass coaching event and spoke with certainty and conviction. The third person on the call seemed to regard her with admiration. I felt my blood pressure rising because my friend owed me a substantial amount of money, which was overdue by a year, and the little I had gotten back was due to my prodding. I knew that my friend was as much a manifesting maven as I was a skilled debt collector.

Over the next few weeks, my friend continued to boast about her manifestation abilities, and I correspondingly stepped up my efforts to get my money back. She ended up sending me a long letter, written in exquisite penmanship, expressing her gratitude for the loan and saying that she would do something special for me "someday." The gist of the letter was that if she happened to come into the money to repay the loan she would, but she wasn't going to go out of her way to make it happen. She didn't apologize for the delay or inconvenience. She instead blamed it on the economic downturn caused by the pandemic, even though the loan was supposed to have been repaid before the pandemic began. She also mentioned working long hours on her non-profit, implying she had more important things to do. It was basically a long-winded, ornate blowoff.

Later that day, I was at the beach watching pelicans dive for fish. There were numerous seagulls in the mix, and every time a pelican emerged with a fish in its bill several seagulls attempted to steal it. The idea popped into my head to google this behavior, and I learned it was called kleptoparasitism, which is "a form of parasitism in which an animal steals food or objects collected, caught, prepared, or stored by another animal."[6] It is a survival strategy when stealing food is less costly than trying to directly attain it for oneself. It reminded me of my friend's behavior. Even though she hadn't stolen my money, she had made false promises and unapologetically left me dangling. She had also tried to involve me in a few of her get-rich-quick schemes. In light of her continued bragging, I planned to hold her accountable.

As I watched the pelicans dive for fish, I could practically hear the seagulls boasting about their manifestation abilities as they grabbed at the pelicans' catches. I felt an internal shift about my situation, and the next steps became clear. I decided to sue my friend, but I would give her one more chance before proceeding. I told her it was unacceptable to put me off indefinitely, and I asked for a due date for the full repayment of the loan. I didn't mention that I was planning to sue her. To my surprise, she responded immediately, saying she would pay the loan in full, plus 20 percent, in six months. I believed she was sincere, and I felt a tremendous weight lifted.

Meanwhile, things were going smoothly at work. Then, one day, there was big news: the startup had been acquired for $500 million! It was a testament to the sales prowess of the CEO. Employees were celebrating and some planned to buy homes after cashing in their options. My windfall was relatively low, but it moved me from the low income bracket to the moderate income bracket for the year.

When I joined the startup, I didn't known how much equity was standard to receive, and it was difficult to research based on job title. Data jobs didn't have standard titles. On top of that, the job title of the position I applied for was different from the job title in my offer letter, which ended up being different from my actual role. A wise woman pointed out to me that it was still my responsibility to research the topic, which was true. After talking to her, I read that in Silicon Valley "female employees earn just 47 cents of equity for every $1 of equity a male employee earns."[7] I vowed that if I ever worked in a startup again, I would ask for twice as much equity as I was offered.

The CEO of the acquiring company met with the startup to introduce himself, provide the company's history, and explain why they decided to acquire us. He was highly energetic and enthusiastic, and his style seemed aligned with that of traditional tech leaders. He mentioned in passing that he was a proponent of Ayn Rand's philosophy, which rejected things I believed in, like intuition and regulations in capitalism. This was nothing new in tech, but I had hoped the pandemic and other world events would have inspired leaders to shift away from such extreme beliefs.

Albert Einstein and Steve Jobs credited their success to intuition, and I wished the tech industry would have evolved to start experimenting with it. Why not consider what intuition had to say in conjunction with the other inputs into the decision-making processes at tech companies? From a data standpoint, I believed that intuition tapped into information far more comprehensive, accurate, and unbiased than what could be collected with the five senses. I didn't understand how intuition worked, but I trusted in its integrity.

Employees were told that the acquisition wouldn't affect day-to-day operations for several months, which was welcome news to me. I mentally prepared myself for another job search and kept an open mind about the timing. In the meantime, I was happy in my role and planned to enjoy it while it lasted.

In June 2021, the startup provided tickets to an online women-in-technology conference in which Michelle Obama was the keynote interview. Unfortunately, the conference itself ended up being a fiasco because the streaming platform crashed. The comments section of the platform still worked, however, and a steady flow of scathing remarks poured in. The situation ironically captured how little women in tech support each other (I provided my own experience of this in an earlier chapter), and why the conference was needed in the first place.

A couple of days later, Michelle Obama's interview was replayed and I was able to tune in. The part of her interview that felt especially relevant and inspiring to me was when she talked about the importance of balance and knowing your worth. She mentioned that after she gave birth to Sasha, she went from working full time to three days a week. After a while, she realized that she was producing as much as she had working five days a week but wasn't getting paid for it. She then switched to a new job that was three days a week in which she received full-time pay, and thereafter limited her engagements and projects to three days a week as much as possible. I knew that the work I was doing during my three-day work week was worth more than the low income I was getting paid, yet I hadn't dared to dream bigger because I was already getting flak from co-workers. Michelle Obama showed me what was possible, and I knew the time had come for me to leave the startup. Sometime later I remembered that I had intuitively chosen her picture for the center of my last collage at the art studio, and it made me smile.

Whatever my next job was, I hoped that the representation of women was better. I found the lack of progress in this area over the course of my career discouraging and frustrating. In the United States, the percentage of women in computing jobs had declined from 32 percent to 25 percent since 1990. The percentage of women in engineering jobs had increased, but from only 12 percent to 15 percent.[8] Like many women before me, I had had enough of the same old story.

The startup had a women-in-technology group that solicited ideas from female employees for talks and activities. I proposed a couple of times to create an anonymous survey to identify issues female employees encountered in the startup and ideas for potential solutions that I would collate and present, but the group voted to learn Excel spreadsheet short-cuts and best practices for presentations, make bookmarks, and do yoga instead. These were all valuable ways to help each other succeed, but avoided the elephant in the room. How would the gender gap close unless we talked about it?

At one of the group's meetings, the CEO encouraged female

employees to speak up more about their accomplishments because he noticed that their male counterparts did so freely. I thought it was fantastic that the CEO had taken the time to be with us and offer his perspective. Unfortunately, the advice given to women was usually to behave more like men. Was there also going to be a meeting with the male employees to advise them to behave more like women? Was there awareness that when women did speak up, they were often ignored or dismissed by men? Speaking up only worked if someone was there to listen. The CEO and most of the men I worked with were good listeners, but certain male employees regularly cut me off before I could complete a single sentence or made belittling remarks if I talked about something I had achieved. In contrast, they were chummy and engaging with their male counterparts. Were we going to continue to reward that type of behavior?

One day, the head of the marketing team organized her own women's event that involved a frank conversation about women in tech. It was exactly what I had been wishing for. When she asked me how it felt to have had a long tech career in Silicon Valley as a woman, I realized that nobody had ever asked me that before. It felt liberating to finally be seen and acknowledged, and the meeting was a helpful step for me in getting closure on this part of my career.

I didn't sense it at the time, but this chapter of my life was winding down to a close, both personally and professionally, and the pace was about to pick up.

Almost a year had passed since access to my special redwood tree had been cut off and I still didn't know if the tree had been damaged or to what extent. I saw an advertisement for an art fair in the redwoods with a magnificent image of a redwood scene painted by a local artist. I remembered the artist's work from the previous year's flyer and found it remarkable that she was able to capture the energy of the forest on canvas. I decided to buy three giclee prints from her collection to bring the forest into my apartment since I wasn't able to go to it. One of the prints reminded me of the energetic experience with my tree.

A few days before the prints were delivered, I found out that access to my redwood tree had been restored! I jumped into my car and headed straight over. When I arrived in the general vicinity, the forest was mostly intact but the vibrant energy was gone. I felt a hollow emptiness as I drove along the road and wondered if the forest was experiencing trauma. When I hiked to my tree, I was thrilled to find it nearly unscathed. Only the surface of its bark had been charred and singed on the side facing the source of the fire. Fifty feet ahead, the forest was still closed off. I felt like I had been reunited with a missing family member who had defied the odds. I hugged the tree and cried, but was unable to connect with it again. I came to understand that my relationship with it had come to a close. Maybe the tree had changed too much or maybe the forest had been my version of a Neverland or Narnia and I had changed too much.

The artist dropped off the prints at my apartment, and they were even more magnificent in real life and served as the perfect mementos of the time I had with my tree. I placed the print that reminded me of my energetic experience above my desk as an inspiration for my work. The prints replaced the few remaining landscape photographs taken by my former best friend that were still hanging on my walls. I knew I should have taken down his work years earlier, but I didn't know what to replace it with and thought the barren walls would have been even more depressing to look at.

As if on cue, a few days after I put up the new prints I bumped into my former best friend. We occasionally crossed paths in our small town and the conversation was always the same: he would act like we were pals, I would remind him that he abandoned me and was no pal of mine, and he would blame his girlfriend. This time, however, the conversation ended differently. He took responsibility and apologized for hurting me. In an instant, my angst disappeared and I felt neutral whenever I bumped into him after that. I was grateful to finally move on.

During this time, a fourteen-year-old orange tabby cat, who lived with one of my neighbors but roamed our complex and had become my best friend during the pandemic, got cancer. He used to greet me and other tenants when we pulled into the driveway, and he often visited my apartment. I decided the picture of the monks in my last collage represented my relationship with the cat because we always had a fun time together amid the bleak backdrop of world events.

A couple of days before the cat was to be euthanized, my significant other and I were with him in the courtyard and my "black hole" neighbor came by, got down on her knees, faced the cat, and wailed, "I can't believe this is happening!!!!!!!! I prayed for you day and night for NINE YEARRRRRRRRS!!!!!!!!!!! OH, GODDDDDDDD!!!!!!!!!! OH, GODDDDDDDD!!!!!!!!!!" She screamed at the top of her lungs for a couple of minutes accompanied by a torrent of tears, then stopped on a dime and told me to tell the owner that she'd said goodbye to the cat. Then she resumed screaming and crying for another minute, stopped again, and told me to make sure I told the owner that she'd said goodbye. I was shaken to the core.

My neighbor had openly objected to this particular cat being allowed outdoors, repeatedly discouraged me from interacting with him, and yelled at him multiple times a week for years when he came on her deck. I understood why she didn't want the cat on her deck, but I was flabbergasted by her over-the-top goodbye that was completely at odds with the way she had treated him. She once left me a two-minute voice-mail after the cat had killed a rat and left the remains at the foot of one of the stairwells. She screamed multiple times, "He's a MURDERERRRRRRRR!!!!!!!!!! OH, GODDDDDDD!!!!!!!!!! OH, GODDDDDDDD!!!!!!!!!!" accompanied by intense sobbing. A few days later, I was petting the cat in the courtyard and another tenant came up to me and asked, "Did you know that he's a murderer?" I wondered how many people my neighbor had called.

After more than a decade of dealing with my neighbor, I had had enough. Even her grieving was manipulative. I described her behavior to a therapist, who said it sounded like she was exhibiting several symptoms of vulnerable narcissism (also known as covert narcissism). Vulnerable narcissism is a type of narcissism that embodies unhealthy feminine traits such as passive aggressiveness, anxiety, and whispering campaigns (though, in my neighbor's case, it was more like screaming campaigns). This type of narcissism isn't as well known as grandiose narcissism, which embodies unhealthy masculine traits such as aggression, anger, and direct confrontation.

There was no way to know if my neighbor had narcis-sistic personality disorder without a professional diagnosis, but I googled how to deal with covert narcissism in case there was any helpful advice. The most common recommen-dation I found was to set boundaries and, if possible, create distance or cut off contact entirely with the person. I couldn't create more distance with my neighbor unless I moved out of the complex, which was a prohibitively costly option. In the past I had tried reasoning with her and she ignored or deflected my comments. I had also tried tuning her out and avoiding her with limited success. I decided I was ready to try setting boundaries with her even though I feared retaliation.

When my neighbor tried manipulating me again, I told her that it was not okay to do so and that it affected me. She didn't acknowledge how I felt. Her reaction was to rationalize her behavior with nonsensical lies, deny any wrongdoing, say that she's a respectful person, shift the blame to me, and lie to the landlord. When I proceeded to draw boundaries with her, she gave me the silent treatment, then later changed her story to say she lied for noble reasons, adding that anyone who draws boundaries must have been severely abused as a child and that the landlord agreed with her completely. Then she repeated several times that she is "SO respectful!" Much of her response was gaslighting and even though it was very upsetting to endure, it was worth it to experience less toxicity and duplicity thereafter.

Meanwhile, the day was arriving for my friend from the week-long village to repay the loan. She said she wanted to meet in person to do so. At first I resisted the idea, but then I remembered how much unconditional support she had given me in the past when I really needed it and how she had made it possible for me to attend phenomenal workshops and events. She had been extremely generous to me in many ways. I agreed to see her and hoped it would be like old times.

When we met, she gave me a cashier's check for the remainder of the loan plus 20 percent. I normally wouldn't have accepted a bonus but, in this case, I felt like I had earned it. I was so grateful the loan was repaid and the drama was over! However, during our brief meeting my friend kept repeating that she was amazing at manifesting money. I felt like she was no longer herself but some kind of positive affirmation robot who was impossible to talk to, or maybe she was gaslighting me. I decided to end the friendship.

The following week my job search panned out and I received an offer that felt like a fresh start. It came just in time, as the company culture was shifting and I was becoming more impatient with my colleagues. The position was with the local government for administering and supporting a homeless management information system. The end users included the federally-funded homelessness program providers in my county. I was excited to leave the tech sector for an organization with the goal to end homelessness! It took only twelve job applications to receive the offer.

The day I accepted the offer, I went to the beach. The waves were higher than usual and they closed out, one after the other, with a loud boom and a sheet of mist spraying upward. From where I sat, I saw a rainbow sustained in the succession of mist. It reminded me that over the past couple of years there had been a barrage of collapses in the normal flow of life, which created the conditions for a spectacular spectrum of gifts. My life had changed for the better in so many ways and I felt like I had a lot to look forward to!

During my last two weeks at the startup, my boss posted job listings for two full-time employees to do my role. He had written the descriptions so well that I felt happy butterflies in my stomach when I read them. I was overjoyed that the leader of a big data team recognized the value of a role that was part art, part science in an organization that was typically purely engineering-based. I felt satisfied that I had left a feminine mark in the data pipeline.

The data team did a farewell Zoom call for me, and I was deeply touched. One of the employees in India who was on maternity leave dialed in. The rooftop serenader also joined in, even though he was no longer with the startup; he met up with one of the current employees for the call and I clapped with joy! These were precious surprises.

On my last day, I spoke with the head of equity and diversity at the parent company. I shared what it was like to be a middle-aged woman in a tech company in Silicon Valley. It felt good to let go of my baggage on my way out, and I hoped it might make a difference for other women in the startup.

When I looked back at the past few years, I could see that I had embodied Data for Joy. Turning to intuition, data, and nature's patterns to navigate rapid, extreme change had happened implicitly and automatically. I also thought about the "what ifs." What if I hadn't taken the time after GoPro to learn life skills, create a support system, and formulate a way to stay in balance? I instantly felt knots in my stomach and knew the outcome would have been very ugly. What if I had moved to Oregon? My stomach relaxed. The circumstances probably would have been less challenging, but staying in Silicon Valley allowed me to achieve a sense of completeness and closure of this stage of my life that wouldn't have been possible if I had walked away. It also gave me the opportunity to stress-test Data for Joy in extreme conditions and know that it worked for me.

As I sat on my couch, which I had become overly familiar with during the pandemic, I checked to see how my body felt in the present moment. It was relaxed but strong, and there was a light, tingly flutter of excitement in my stomach. I felt like a new person.

CHAPTER 6
CLOSING

The online world is now in its third generation, Web 3.0, which includes generative AI (artificial intelligence algorithms that generate text, video, etc.). Generative AI adds another layer of convenience, and projection, to consumer content experiences by synthesizing information into a unique output in the user's format of choice, such as a story or poem. The potential is tremendous, but so is the need for vigilance by consumers. Popular generative AI tools source information from the internet, which includes untruths and inaccuracies. Furthermore, synthesizing information via algorithms can undercut human originality and critical thinking.

The evolving role of algorithms in serving content to consumers is illustrated in Figure 7.

Looking back, early Web 2.0 is when the tech industry took a sharp turn for the worse for me as an employee and a consumer. Sometimes I refer to Web 2.0 as web double whammy because it delivered a one-two punch. First, new platforms opened up content creation to anyone, giving rise to "fake news" and the "selfie" culture.

Second, the role of algorithms in serving personalized content meant that groups of people no longer shared the same projections of reality; each person was served their own variation, leading to disagreements. Algorithms viewed disagreements as "engaging" and perpetuated the dynamics. The efforts to address these issues are ongoing.

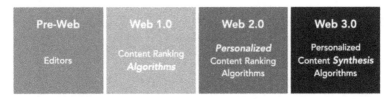

Figure 7. The Evolving Role of Algorithms in Serving Content to Consumers

While Web 3.0 inherits the information integrity issues of Web 2.0, it redirects consumers to creative endeavors, which feels like a big step in the right direction. Some AI tools allow consumers and workplaces to upload their own information sources, giving them control over the integrity of the inputs. The iPhone's new Journal app provides consumers with intelligent prompts from the information on their phone in a private experience designed to increase gratitude, presence, and purpose. I think Steve Jobs would have approved.

One of the other impacts of Web 3.0 is that it opens the door to integrating AI into more workplace operations, leading to shifting job responsibilities as well as job losses, unfortunately. For example, going back to the analogy in Chapter 1 of comparing a data pipeline to a food pipeline, with Web 3.0 it's no longer just an analogy. Silicon Valley startup CloudChef uses generative AI to "serve Michelin-like dishes, with untrained staff [and] superhuman consistency [by] codify[ing] the intuition of the chef."[1] They provide royalties to the chefs who create the recipes they use, so it's a mutually beneficial relationship. If adopted, however, the technology could shift the balance of power among chefs across the world, and some chefs would increase their reach while others would be displaced. The question is whether comfort food is as comforting when the preparation is orchestrated by a computer in the kitchen?

While the impact of algorithms on our social lives, work-places, and consumer experiences is concerning, an even bigger issue, in my opinion, is monopolies in the online world. For example, at the time of writing, Google is facing an antitrust lawsuit for establishing a search monopoly. The CEO of Microsoft has testified that Google's monopoly gives it a huge advantage in the generative AI competition, which creates a "nightmare" scenario for the balance of power in the online world.[2] I agree. It feels critical to reinstate competition in the online world now that it's so pervasive in our day-to-day lives.

It has been more than thirty years since the birth of the web, and Tim Berners-Lee believes it has gone astray with too much power and personal data in the hands of a few organiza-tions. His vision for restoring balance to his creation is to give consumers more power in the form of pods (personal online data stores) in which each person could control their own data and companies could only access it with their permission. "The long view is a thriving decentralized marketplace, fueled by personal empowerment and collaboration."[3]

This is a unifying vision that consumers can help bring to fruition by acting from a place of empowerment and collabora-tion right now. There are countless ways to do so, many of which are free: spend less time online, write to your legislators, meditate, shop more often in physical stores, host in-person gatherings, reach out to people in your life who are addicted to their phones, click with intention, hone your intuition, hug trees, slow down, grow your own vegetables, support artists, share your story, go on a hike, start your own conscious business, process your emotions, draw healthy boundaries, do a sit spot, reconnect with your soul, listen for your next steps and follow them.

The good news is that systemic measures are finally being taken to directly address the harmful effects of algorithms. President Biden signed an Executive Order on "safe, secure, and trustworthy artificial intelligence."[4] Hollywood actors went on strike for 118 days and reached a deal that included AI protections. Google employees have organized a union whose mission includes making sure Google acts ethically and for public good, though fewer than 1 percent of Google's 180,000 employees are members.[5] Thirty-three states, including California, are suing Facebook for contributing to the youth mental health crisis. I feel hopeful that as more people across the globe start chipping away at the problem from different angles, it will crack wide open and bring humanity closer together in the process. After all, we humans have superpowers that algorithms do not, like compassion, ingenuity, and love.

EPILOGUE

After leaving the startup, a new set of challenging circumstances came into my life and I ended up leaving the government job. When things stabilized, I had a persistent feeling that there was something I was supposed to do, but I didn't know what it was. One day, a teacher recommended that I write a book about my story in the tech industry. The suggestion immediately felt right to me, even though I find writing excruciating. I jumped in and began. However, I felt uncomfortable and vulnerable staying with the process, not just because it was emotionally taxing and far slower than I had imagined, but because our culture doesn't allow us to pause.

Towards the end of the project, I turned on the news and saw that Simone Biles, the most decorated gymnast in history, had just won the balance beam and floor exercise gold medals at the 2023 Gymnastics World Championships. What I found most inspiring about her wins was that she had only recently returned to competing after a nearly two-year hiatus that started when she developed "the twisties," a condition in which an athlete's mind and body become out of sync.[1][1] By allowing herself the time she needed, she came back as the most balanced woman on the planet! She said, "I had to prove to myself that I could still get out here, twist, I could prove all the haters wrong that I'm not a quitter, this, that, the other."[2] Her example helped me trust in my own hiatus, and I hoped that such life intermissions would be commonplace someday, lest humanity fall into a perpetual state of the twisties.

Soon afterwards I had the realization that my next step with using data for joy was to train decision-makers on how to leverage data to achieve their goals, especially in organizations trying to create positive change in the world. Nowadays, even spiritual and philanthropic organizations use analytics, but there is a data literacy gap in realizing its fullest potential. I also sensed there were leaders who were ready and open to learn.

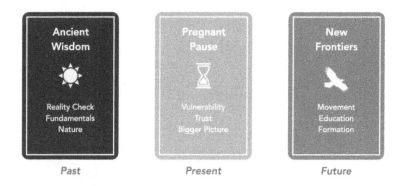

Figure 8. My Journey to Restore Balance in the Age of Algorithms

I depicted my journey using a "past, present, future spread," which is a three-card layout I learned from the oracle card framework, illustrated in Figure 8.

A couple of days after creating the spread, I was contacted

about a part-time data consulting opportunity with a non-profit in the education sector that closely matched my "future" card. I joined the project and knew I was exactly where I was supposed to be. After years of preparation and waiting, it was time to fly.

QUESTIONS FOR READERS AND BOOK CLUBS

1. What is your biggest takeaway from the book?
2. Which parts of the book can you most relate to? Least relate to?
3. Which parts of the book do you wish went deeper?
4. What is your relationship with the online world? Is there anything you will do differently after reading the book?
5. If you have a smartphone, what are the apps you use most and how much time do you spend on them?
6. If you owned a social media site, what criteria would you ideally use to sort content in consumers' feeds or to recommend new content?
7. How do you think algorithms be used to bring more joy to the world? How can you apply these ideas to what you put out into the world?
8. What do you think is the sexiest job of the 21st century?

9. How much do you rely on intuition versus logic when making decisions?

10. What are some examples of data-driven decisions you made today?

11. What major challenges have you overcome, and how did you do it? Have you shared your wisdom with anybody?

12. What is your relationship with nature? Have you ever communicated with flora or fauna?

13. How well does the mental health system in your area meet the community's needs? Do you know who to call if a loved one is experiencing a mental health crisis?

14. What were your perceptions of the tech industry before reading this book? Did anything change after reading the book?

15. How much of your life has been "before web" and "after web"? What are the top pros and cons of each era?

16. What ideas do you have for restoring balance to the online world?

17. What do you think of the expanding capabilities of algorithms from Web 1.0 through 3.0? What do you think algorithms will be able to do in future generations of the web?

ACKNOWLEDGMENTS

Thank you to my family, Ames, Barbara, Cathy, Geri, Jean, Julianna, my landlord, Patrick, Peggy, Raz, and Renee.

ABOUT THE AUTHOR

Phylis Savari has been a data professional for three decades. Her goal in writing this memoir is to inspire consumers and creators of data-driven products to make choices that elevate the level of joy in the world.

BIBLIOGRAPHY

1. AWARENESS

Adi Robertson (December 22, 2011). The Verge. Yahoo on Facebook gets 'persistent state of sharing' with new sites and notifications. Yahoo is adding 26 sites to Facebook's Open Graph after seeing a 300 percent increase in news site traffic from Facebook in the US. A new notifications feature will also show users their friends' activities across Yahoo sites. Retrieved December 2023 from https://www.theverge.com/2011/12/22/2653856/yahoo-facebook-integration-new-sites-open-graph

Altaba (February 24, 2009). News Release. Yahoo! Introduces New Ad Products to Help Marketers Reach Audiences With Greater Precision. Retrieved December 2023 from https://www.altaba.com/news-releases/news-release-details/yahoo-introduces-new-ad-products-help-marketers-reach-audiences

Altaba (June 5, 1996). News Release. Yahoo! To Feature Digital's Altavista Search Service In Its Internet Guide. Retrieved December 2023 from https://www.altaba.com/news-releases/news-release-details/yahoo-feature-digitals-altavista-search-service-its-internet

Amazon Press Release (March 14, 2006). Amazon Web Services Launches. Retrieved December 2023 from https://press.aboutamazon.com/2006/3/amazon-web-services-launches

Apache Hadoop (July 2008). July 2008 - Hadoop Wins Terabyte Sort Benchmark. Retrieved December 2023 from https://hadoop.apache.org/news/2008-07-xx-terabyte-sort.html

BBC News (March 17, 2008). Microsoft's moves 'threaten net'. Any deal between Yahoo and Microsoft could be "bad for the internet", according to the head of Google. Retrieved December 2023 from http://news.bbc.co.uk/2/hi/technology/7300337.stm

Brian Cantoni (May 16, 2007). Wikimedia. U.S. Country music singer Taylor Swift performing at Yahoo headquarters. Retrieved December 2023 from https://commons.wikimedia.org/wiki/File:Taylor_Swift_at_Yahoo_crop.jpg

BusinessWeek (May 15, 2006). Mickey D's McMakeover. The heavy plastic look is history. A clean, simple design is on the way in. Retrieved December 2023 from https://web.archive.org/web/20060524233252/http://www.businessweek.com/magazine/content/06_20/b3984065.htm

CERN. A short history of the Web. Retrieved December 2023 from https://home.cern/science/computing/birth-web/short-history-web

Chanchal Singh, Manish Kumar. Mastering Hadoop 3: Big data processing at scale to unlock unique business insights. Packt publishing. Journey to Hadoop 3 (chapter). Hadoop Origins and Timelines (chapter section). Retrieved December 2023 from https://subscription.packtpub.com/book/data/9781788620444/1/ch01lvl1sec10/hadoop-origins-and-timelines

Chris Isidore of CNNMoney.com, Michal Lev-Ram of Fortune (February 1, 2008). Microsoft bids $45 billion for Yahoo. Software giant offers $31 a share - a 62% premium - in deal that could reorder online ad market. Microsoft's Ballmer: 'Major milestone.' Retrieved December 2023 from https://money.cnn.com/2008/02/01/technology/microsoft_yahoo/

Chris Nuttall (July 10, 1998). Inktomi searches for Net profits in Europe. Retrieved December 2023 from http://news.bbc.co.uk/1/hi/business/128974.stm

Comscore (February 5, 2008). Press Release. Media Advisory: Microsoft Bids on Yahoo!. Retrieved December 2023 from https://www.comscore.com/Insights/Press-Releases/2008/02/Microsoft-Bids-on-Yahoo

Comscore (July 12, 2007). Press Release. 772 Million People Online Worldwide in May. Online Retail and E-Commerce Sites Boosted by Holiday Spending. Retrieved December 2023 from https://www.comscore.com/Insights/Press-Releases/2007/07/Top-Worldwide-Web-Properties

Comscore (May 4, 2006). Press Release. 694 Million People Currently Use the Internet Worldwide According To Comscore Networks. Retrieved December 2023 from https://www.comscore.com/Insights/Press-Releases/2006/05/comScore-Launches-World-Metrix

CRN Australia (April 20, 2010). Yahoo hires Blake Irving as chief product officer. Retrieved December 2023 from https://www.crn.com.au/news/yahoo-hires-blake-irving-as-chief-product-officer-172579

Dan Tynan (March 21, 2018). Fast Company. The history of Yahoo, and how it went from phenom to has-been. For one brief shining moment, Yahoo was the king of all it surveyed. Then everything went to hell. Retrieved December 2023 from https://www.fastcompany.com/40544277/the-glory-that-was-yahoo

Dana Blankenhorn (August 10, 2009). ZDNet. Cutting out for Cloudera just in time. It's a well-considered, mature move from a well-considered, mature man. Cutting has been involved in search technology for over two decades, since long before the Web was spun. He was a whiz kid. Now he's a wise man. Retrieved December 2023 from https://www.zdnet.com/article/cutting-out-for-cloudera-just-in-time/

DataCamp (March 2022). Cloudera Hadoop Tutorial. Learn about Hadoop ecosystem, the architectures and how to start with Cloudera. Retrieved

December 2023 from https://www.datacamp.com/tutorial/tutorial-cloud era-hadoop-tutorial

David Goldman (July 29, 2009). CNN Money. Microsoft and Yahoo: Search partners. After a year and a half of dealing, the tech giants reach a 10-year deal to take on Google, which holds a 65% market share in online search. Retrieved December 2023 from https://money.cnn.com/2009/07/29/tech nology/microsoft_yahoo/

Dawn Kawamoto (May 21, 2008). CNET. Microsoft and Yahoo re-enter talks. Microsoft announced Sunday afternoon it has issued another proposal to Yahoo that calls for an acquisition of some but not all of Yahoo's assets. Retrieved December 2023 from https://www.cnet.com/culture/microsoft-and-yahoo-re-enter-talks/

Department of Justice (May 18, 1998). Press Release. JUSTICE DEPARTMENT FILES ANTITRUST SUIT AGAINST MICROSOFT FOR UNLAWFULLY MONOPOLIZING COMPUTER SOFTWARE MARKETS. Action Would Give Consumers More Choices 20 State Attorneys General and the District of Columbia File Similar Lawsuit. Retrieved December 2023 from https://web. archive.org/web/20090601034720/http://www.usdoj.gov/atr/public/ press_releases/1998/1764.htm

Department of Justice (November 5, 2008). Press Release. Yahoo! Inc. and Google Inc. Abandon Their Advertising Agreement. Resolves Justice Department's Antitrust Concerns, Competition Is Preserved in Markets for Internet Search Advertising. Retrieved December 2023 from https://www. justice.gov/archive/opa/pr/2008/November/08-at-981.html

Donald Miner (August 23, 2016). O'Reilly Media. Hadoop: What you need to know. Learn about the basics of how Hadoop works, why it's such an important technology, and how you should be using it without getting mired in the details. Retrieved December 2023 from https://www.oreilly. com/content/hadoop-what-you-need-to-know/

Doug Gross (November 17, 2009). CNN. Dictionary word of the year: 'Unfriend'. Retrieved December 2023 from https://www.cnn.com/ 2009/TECH/11/17/unfriend.word/index.html

Elinor Mills (December 6, 2005). CNET. Yahoo says 'Let's Groove'. Retrieved December 2023 from https://www.cnet.com/culture/yahoo-says-lets-groove/

Elinor Mills (January 30, 2008). CNET. Yahoo to lay off 1,000 as profit drops. The Internet company says it will lay off 1,000 in February after reporting lower net profit and higher revenue for the fourth quarter. Retrieved December 2023 from https://www.cnet.com/culture/yahoo-to-lay-off-1000-as-profit-drops/

GeeksforGeeks. Introduction to Hadoop. Retrieved December 2023 from https://www.geeksforgeeks.org/hadoop-an-introduction/

Google News Announcement (June 26, 2000). Yahoo! Selects Google as its Default Search Engine Provider. Yahoo! to Integrate Google's Advanced Search Technology into Yahoo!'s Network of Properties. Retrieved December 2023 from https://googlepress.blogspot.com/2000/06/yahoo-selects-google-as-its-default.html

Google Official Blog (July 25, 2008). We knew the web was big... Retrieved December 2023 from https://googleblog.blogspot.com/2008/07/we-knew-web-was-big.html

Hal Plotkin (April 11, 1996). Metro, Silicon Valley's Newspaper. A Couple of Yahoos. Retrieved December 2023 from https://www.metroactive.com/papers/metro/04.11.96/yahoo-9615.html

Ina Fried (February 1, 2008). CNET. Microsoft bids $44.6 billion for Yahoo. Offer--described by Yahoo as "unsolicited"--amounts to $31 per share, or a 62 percent premium above its closing stock price Thursday. Retrieved December 2023 from https://www.cnet.com/tech/tech-industry/microsoft-bids-44-6-billion-for-yahoo/

Ina Fried (July 29, 2009). CNET. Yahoo, Microsoft reach search, ad deal. Under the pact, Microsoft's technology will power Yahoo's search results, while Yahoo will handle ad-selling duties for both companies' search sites. Retrieved December 2023 from https://www.cnet.com/culture/yahoo-microsoft-reach-search-ad-deal-10298303/

Internet Live Stats. Total number of Websites. Retrieved December 2023 from https://www.internetlivestats.com/total-number-of-websites/

James Niccolai (February 19, 2003). Computerworld. Overture to buy AltaVista for $140 million. Retrieved December 2023 from https://www.computerworld.com/article/2581421/overture-to-buy-altavista-for--140-million.html

Jason Kincaid (April 22, 2010). TechCrunch. EdgeRank: The Secret Sauce That Makes Facebook's News Feed Tick. Retrieved December 2023 from https://techcrunch.com/2010/04/22/facebook-edgerank/

Jay Hoffman (February 18, 2020). The Tech: The First Newspaper published online. Retrieved December 2023 from https://thehistoryoftheweb.com/postscript/the-tech-first-newspaper-published-online/

Jayson Derrick (July 25, 2016). Benzinga via Yahoo! Finance. Remember When Yahoo Turned Down $1 Million To Buy Google?. Retrieved December 2023 from https://finance.yahoo.com/news/remember-yahoo-turned-down-1-132805083.html

Jim Hu (February 18, 2004). CNET News. Yahoo dumps Google search technology. Yahoo drops Google as the default search technology provider for its U.S.-based sites, signaling the beginning of the end for the Web's most high-profile marriage of convenience. Retrieved December 2023 from https://www.cnet.com/tech/tech-industry/yahoo-dumps-google-search-technology/

Jim Hu (March 20, 2003). CNET News. Yahoo seals Inktomi deal. The portal giant completes its purchase of Web search technology company Inktomi, highlighting an intent to boost its own flourishing search business. Retrieved December 2023 from https://www.cnet.com/culture/yahoo-seals-inktomi-deal/

John Ryan (July 31, 2018). DZone. Oracle vs. Hadoop. In this article, we'll explain the differences (and benefits) of both Hadoop and Big Data and how they fit into your data architecture. Retrieved December 2023 from https://dzone.com/articles/oracle-vs-hadoop

Josh Quittner (May 8, 2006). TIME. The 2006 TIME 100. Here's our list of the 100 men and women whose power, talent or moral example is transforming our world. The Flickr Founders. Retrieved December 2023 from https://content.time.com/time/specials/packages/arti cle/0,28804,1975813_1976769_1977357,00.html

Julianne Pepitone (December 14, 2010). CNN Money. Yahoo layoffs: 600 jobs cut in long-rumored move. Retrieved December 2023 from https://money.cnn.com/2010/12/14/technology/yahoo_layoffs/index.htm

Karla Hesterberg (November 29, 2021). HubSpot. A Brief History of Online Advertising. Retrieved December 2023 from https://blog.hubspot.com/marketing/history-of-online-advertising

Kelly Fiveash (December 11, 2008). The Register. Yahoo! waves goodbye to 1,500 workers. 'Layoffs unfortunately unavoidable', says Yang. Retrieved December 2023 from https://www.theregister.com/2008/12/11/yahoo_1500_layoffs_search_biz/

Laurie Kulikowski (July 25, 2016). TheStreet. A History of Yahoo!'s Six CEOs. Here's a brief overlook of each of Yahoo's chief executives through the years. Retrieved December 2023 from https://www.thestreet.com/invest ing/stocks/a-history-of-yahoo-s-six-ceos-html

Louise Story, Miguel Helft (April 14, 2007). New York Times. Google Buys DoubleClick for $3.1 Billion. Retrieved December 2023 from https://www.nytimes.com/2007/04/14/technology/14DoubleClick.html

Matthew Gray of the Massachusetts Institute of Technology (1996). Web Growth Summary. Retrieved December 2023 from https://www.mit.edu/people/mkgray/net/web-growth-summary.html

Merriam-Webster Dictionary. Algorithm. Retrieved December 2023 from https://www.merriam-webster.com/dictionary/algorithm

Michael Arrington (September 6, 2006). TechCrunch. Facebook Users Revolt, Facebook Replies. Retrieved December 2023 from https://techcrunch.com/2006/09/06/facebook-users-revolt-facebook-replies/

Miguel Helft (February 12, 2008). New York Times. Layoffs Across Yahoo — Finally. Retrieved December 2023 from https://archive.nytimes.com/bits.blogs.nytimes.com/2008/02/12/layoffs-across-yahoo-finally/

Miguel Helft (January 22, 2008). New York Times. Hundreds of Layoffs Expected at Yahoo. Retrieved December 2023 from https://www.nytimes.com/2008/01/22/technology/22yahoo.html

Miguel Helft (June 20, 2008). New York Times. At Yahoo, the Exodus Continues. Retrieved December 2023 from https://www.nytimes.com/2008/06/20/technology/20yahoo.html

Miguel Helft (October 21, 2008). New York Times. Yahoo to Cut About 10% of Workers. Retrieved December 2023 from https://www.nytimes.com/2008/10/22/technology/companies/22yahoo.html

Mike Hoefflinger (Apr 16, 2017). Business Insider. Inside Mark Zuckerberg's controversial decision to turn down Yahoo's $1 billion early offer to buy Facebook. Retrieved December 2023 from https://www.businessinsider.com/why-mark-zuckerberg-turned-down-yahoos-1-billion-offer-to-buy-facebook-in-2006-2017-4

O'Reilly Media. Mike Olson. Retrieved December 2023 from https://www.oreilly.com/people/mike-olson

Point Reyes National Seashore. National Park Service. Tule Elk. Retrieved December 2023 from https://www.nps.gov/pore/learn/nature/tule_elk.htm

Public Relations Office, School of Computer Science, Carnegie Mellon University (June 20, 1995). Pittsburgh Company Established Using Lycos Internet Catalog Technology. Retrieved December 2023 from https://www.cs.cmu.edu/~./scsnews/jun20-95.html

Rebecca Greenfield (September 21, 2012). The Atlantic via Yahoo! News. Frictionless Sharing Hits the Skids at Facebook. Retrieved December 2023 from https://www.yahoo.com/news/facebook-hits-skids-frictionless-sharing-143235439.html

Reuters (July 30, 2009). Microsoft, Yahoo in Web search partnership. Retrieved December 2023 from https://www.reuters.com/article/uk-microsoft-yahoo-sb/microsoft-yahoo-in-web-search-partnership-idUK TRE56T1A520090730

Reuters (September 17, 2007). FACTBOX: Microsoft's legal troubles in EU, U.S., Asia. Retrieved December 2023 from https://www.reuters.com/article/us-microsoft-eu-troubles/factbox-microsofts-legal-troubles-in-eu-u-s-asia-idUSL0114773220070917

Richard Feloni (January 21, 2015). Business Insider via Yahoo! Finance. Steve Jobs Used This Simple Productivity Hack To Hone Apple's Focus. Retrieved December 2023 from https://finance.yahoo.com/news/steve-jobs-used-simple-productivity-175545445.html

Ruchi Sanghvi (September 5, 2006). The Facebook Blog. Facebook Gets a Facelift. Retrieved December 2023 from https://web.archive.org/web/20101114112237/http://blog.facebook.com/blog.php?post=2207967130

Ryan Singel (June 8, 2010). WIRED. Facebook Comes to Yahoo, But Yahoo Not Going Away. Retrieved December 2023 from https://www.wired.com/2010/06/facebook-yahoo/

Scott Moritz (April 10, 2008). CNN Money. Yahoo turns to Google for help. Internet search giant explores possibility of giving ad space to rival Google in its latest move to fend off a hostile bid by Microsoft. Retrieved December 2023 from https://money.cnn.com/2008/04/09/technology/moritz_yahoo_google.fortune/?postversion=2008041008

Sean Michael Kerner (February 13, 2023). TechTarget. Web 2.0 vs. Web 3.0 vs. Web 1.0: What's the difference? Retrieved December 2023 from https://www.techtarget.com/whatis/feature/Web-20-vs-Web-30-Whats-the-difference

Seeking Alpha (April 18, 2006). Yahoo! Q1 2006 Earnings Call Transcript. Retrieved December 2023 from https://seekingalpha.com/article/9173-yahoo-q1-2006-earnings-call-transcript

Stefanie Olsen (July 14, 2003). CNET News. Yahoo to buy Overture for $1.63 billion. The Web portal says it plans to buy search company Overture Services, a move that's squarely aimed at taking on Google, MSN and other search engine competitors. Retrieved December 2023 from https://www.cnet.com/tech/tech-industry/yahoo-to-buy-overture-for-1-63-billion/

Stephen Shankland (April 21, 2009). CNET. Yahoo plans layoff after profit plunges. Several hundred employees will lose jobs in coming weeks as the online pioneer tries to change course. Retrieved December 2023 from https://www.cnet.com/tech/services-and-software/yahoo-plans-layoff-after-profit-plunges/

Stephen Shankland (June 16, 2008). CNET. Yahoo inks search ad pact with Google. Google will supply Yahoo with search ads in a partnership Yahoo believes will raise revenue by $800 million in its first year--but that also could give more power to Google. Retrieved December 2023 from https://www.cnet.com/culture/yahoo-inks-search-ad-pact-with-google/

Stephen Shankland (May 8, 2008). CNET. Google addresses antitrust issue on Yahoo ad deal. Microsoft is concerned an ad deal with Yahoo would extend Google's search-ad dominance. Google execs says people should look at the bigger ad market. Retrieved December 2023 from https://www.cnet.com/culture/google-addresses-antitrust-issue-on-yahoo-ad-deal/

Stephen Shankland (November 18, 2008). CNET. Yahoo CEO Yang to step down. Jerry Yang will step back to his chief Yahoo role as soon as a successor is found for the CEO role, Yahoo announces. Retrieved December 2023 from https://www.cnet.com/tech/services-and-software/yahoo-ceo-yang-to-step-down/

Steve Lohr (May 5, 2008). New York Times. Microsoft's Failed Yahoo Bid Risks Online Growth. Retrieved December 2023 from https://www.nytimes.com/

2008/05/05/technology/05soft.html

Steven Schwankert (April 30, 2007). Network World. Yahoo buys remainder of Right Media for $680 million. Retrieved December 2023 from https://www.networkworld.com/article/2298584/yahoo-buys-remainder-of-right-media-for--680-million.html

Steven Schwankert (February 14, 2008). InfoWorld. Yahoo sends letter to shareholders over Microsoft bid. CEO Jerry Yang says Yahoo wants to take advantage of a 'unique window of time' in the growth of online ads to build market share and create value for stockholders. Retrieved December 2023 from https://www.infoworld.com/article/2642555/yahoo-sends-letter-to-shareholders-over-microsoft-bid.html

TechCrunch (July 26, 2007). Microsoft Acquires Advertising Exchange Platform AdECN. Retrieved December 2023 from https://techcrunch.com/2007/07/26/microsoft-acquires-advertising-exchange-platform-adecn/

The Associated Press via NBC News (January 13, 2009). Yahoo names technology veteran new CEO. Yahoo Inc. named Silicon Valley veteran Carol Bartz as its new chief executive Tuesday, bringing in a no-nonsense leader known for developing a clear focus. Retrieved December 2023 from https://www.nbcnews.com/id/wbna28640438

The Associated Press via NBC News (Oct. 9, 2006). Google buys YouTube for $1.65 billion. Google Inc. is snapping up YouTube Inc. for $1.65 billion in a deal that catapults the Internet search leader to a starring role in the online video revolution. Retrieved December 2023 from https://www.nbcnews.com/id/wbna15196982

The History of SEO. Short History of Early Search Engines. Retrieved December 2023 from https://web.archive.org/web/20190121213229/http://www.thehistoryofseo.com/The-Industry/Short_History_of_Early_Search_Engines.aspx

Wikipedia. Carol Bartz. Retrieved December 2023 from https://en.wikipedia.org/wiki/Carol_Bartz#CEO_of_Yahoo!

Wikipedia. What Happens Here, Stays Here. Retrieved December 2023 from https://en.wikipedia.org/wiki/What_Happens_Here,_Stays_Here

Wikipedia. List of websites founded before 1995. Retrieved December 2023 from https://en.wikipedia.org/wiki/List_of_websites_founded_before_1995

Wikipedia. Mosaic (web browser). Retrieved December 2023 from https://en.wikipedia.org/wiki/Mosaic_(web_browser)

Wikipedia. Page Rank. Retrieved December 2023 from https://en.wikipedia.org/wiki/PageRank

Wikipedia. World Wide Web Worm. Retrieved December 2023 from https://en.wikipedia.org/wiki/World_Wide_Web_Worm

Wikipedia. Yahoo! 360°. Retrieved December 2023 from https://en.wikipedia.org/wiki/Yahoo!_360%C2%B0

Wikipedia. Yahoo! Photos. Retrieved December 2023 from https://en.wiki pedia.org/wiki/Yahoo!_Photos

Wikipedia. Yahoo!. https://en.wikipedia.org/wiki/Yahoo!

WIRED (July 19, 2000). Why CNET Bought ZDNet. Retrieved December 2023 from https://wired.com/2000/07/why-cnet-bought-zdnet/amp

2. AWAKENING

Alfred Ng (February 21, 2017). CNET. Verizon scrapes $350 million off deal to buy Yahoo. After its disclosures about massive security breaches, Yahoo apparently wasn't worth the original $4.83 billion price tag. Retrieved December 2023 from https://www.cnet.com/tech/tech-industry/verizon-and-yahoo-agree-to-cut-4-billion-deal-by-350-million/

Alzheimer's Association, Research and Progress. Can Alzheimer's Disease Be Prevented? Retrieved December 2023 from https://www.alz.org/alzheimers-dementia/research_progress/prevention

Amaya Taylor (February 16, 2022). Housing Matters, an Urban Institute Initiative. Millions of Americans Live Near Toxic Waste Sites. How Does This Affect Their Health? Retrieved December 2023 from https://housing matters.urban.org/articles/millions-americans-live-near-toxic-waste-sites-how-does-affect-their-health

Andrew Nusca (July 5, 2012). ZDNet. Microsoft has 'become the thing they despised'. There's a new feature about Microsoft in Vanity Fair this month. It's called "Microsoft's Lost Decade." Uh oh. Retrieved December 2023 from https://www.zdnet.com/article/microsoft-has-become-the-thing-they-despised/

Angela Howe (October 1, 2018). Surfrider Foundation. U.S. Supreme Court Finalizes Win for Martin's Beach Access! Retrieved December 2023 from https://www.surfrider.org/news/us-supreme-court-finalizes-win-for-martins-beach-access

Autism Speaks. What Is Asperger Syndrome? Retrieved December 2023 from https://www.autismspeaks.org/types-autism-what-asperger-syndrome

BBC News (March 12, 2011). Japan earthquake: Tsunami reaches US West Coast. Retrieved December 2023 from https://www.bbc.com/news/world-us-canada-12714558

Business Insider via Financial Post (December 21, 2012). Yahoo employees don't approve of Marissa Mayer as much as they used to. Marissa Mayer's approval ratings among Yahoo employees have dropped 17% since her first quarter as CEO. Retrieved December 2023 from https://financialpost.com/business-insider/yahoo-employees-dont-approve-of-marissa-mayer-as-much-as-they-used-to

Cade Metz (July 10, 2008). The Register. Cokeheads slip AI onto Yahoo! front

page. Optimizing Britney. Retrieved December 2023 from https://www.
theregister.com/2008/07/10/yahoo_front_page_ai/

California Department of Conservation. Tōhoku-oki Earthquake and Tsunami
(March 11, 2011). Retrieved December 2023 from https://www.conserva
tion.ca.gov/cgs/tsunami/tohoku

California Department of Parks and Recreation. The Forest of Nisene Marks
State Park. Retrieved December 2023 from https://www.parks.ca.gov/?
page_id=666

CNBC (May 3, 2012). Letter From Third Point to Yahoo Board Challenging
CEO's Credentials. Retrieved December 2023 from https://www.cnbc.com/
2012/05/03/letter-from-third-point-to-yahoo-board-challenging-ceos-
credentials.html

Danny Sullivan (April 20, 2011). The Yahoo Search Revenue Disaster. Retrieved
December 2023 from https://searchengineland.com/the-yahoo-search-
revenue-disaster-73868

Department of Psychology. Harvard University. Timothy Leary, (1920-1996)
The Effects of Psychotropic Drugs. Retrieved December 2023 from https://
psychology.fas.harvard.edu/people/timothy-leary

E.B. Boyd (August 1, 2011). Fast Company. Brains And Bots Deep Inside Yahoo's
CORE Grab A Billion Clicks. Retrieved December 2023 from https://www.
fastcompany.com/1770673/brains-and-bots-deep-inside-yahoos-core-
grab-billion-clicks

Earthquake Hazards Program (June 8, 2023). United States Geological Survey.
San Francisco Bay Area Liquefaction Hazard Maps. Retrieved December
2023 from https://www.usgs.gov/programs/earthquake-hazards/science/
san-francisco-bay-area-liquefaction-hazard-maps

Gary Strauss (April 30, 2013). USA Today. Yahoo's Mayer got $36.6 million in
2012 compensation. Retrieved December 2023 from https://www.usato
day.com/story/money/business/2013/04/30/yahoo-discloses-marissa-
mayers-2012-compensation/2125059/

Jay Yarow (July 3, 2012). Business Insider. Microsoft Was Destroyed By Its
'Stack Review' Process, According To New Vanity Fair Expose. Retrieved
December 2023 from https://www.businessinsider.com/microsoft-was-
destroyed-by-its-stack-review-process-according-to-new-vanity-fair-
expose-2012-7

Jessica Guynn (April 5, 2012). Los Angeles Times. Yahoo announces 2,000
layoffs as new CEO seeks turnaround. Retrieved December 2023 from
https://www.latimes.com/business/la-xpm-2012-apr-05-la-fi-yahoo-
layoffs-20120405-story.html

Jon Hamilton (April 7, 2011). NPR, Morning Edition. In Japan, Shaken Soil
Turned Soft After Quake. Retrieved December 2023 from https://www.npr.
org/2011/04/07/135181474/in-japan-shaken-soil-turned-soft-after-quake

Julianne Pepitone (February 14, 2012). CNN Money. Activist shareholder Loeb launches Yahoo proxy fight. Retrieved December 2023 from https://money.cnn.com/2012/02/14/technology/yahoo_proxy/index.htm

Julianne Pepitone (February 25, 2013). CNN Money. Marissa Mayer: Yahoos can no longer work from home. Retrieved December 2023 from https://money.cnn.com/2013/02/25/technology/yahoo-work-from-home/index.html

Julianne Pepitone (February 7, 2012). CNN Money. Yahoo board shakeup: Four directors heading out. Retrieved December 2023 from https://money.cnn.com/2012/02/07/technology/yahoo_board/index.htm

Julianne Pepitone (May 14, 2012). CNN Money. Yahoo confirms CEO is out after resume scandal. Retrieved December 2023 from https://money.cnn.com/2012/05/13/technology/yahoo-ceo-out/index.htm

Julianne Pepitone (September 26, 2012). CNN Money. Marissa Mayer's Yahoo turnaround starts to take shape. Retrieved December 2023 from https://money.cnn.com/2012/09/26/technology/yahoo-strategy/index.html

Kyle Chin (November 10, 2023). UpGuard. Biggest Data Breaches in US History [Updated 2023]. Retrieved December 2023 from https://www.upguard.com/blog/biggest-data-breaches-us

Laurie Kulikowski (July 25, 2016). TheStreet. A History of Yahoo!'s Six CEOs. Here's a brief overlook of each of Yahoo's chief executives through the years. Retrieved December 2023 from https://www.thestreet.com/investing/stocks/a-history-of-yahoo-s-six-ceos-html

Metropolitan Transportation Commission, Vital Signs (December 2022). Home Prices. National Context Section. Retrieved December 2023 from https://vitalsigns.mtc.ca.gov/indicators/home-prices

National Centers for Environmental Information, National Oceanic and Atmospheric Administration (March 11, 2023). On This Day: 2011 Tohoku Earthquake and Tsunami. Retrieved December 2023 from https://www.ncei.noaa.gov/news/day-2011-japan-earthquake-and-tsunami

Nicholas Carlson (December 17, 2014). New York Times. What Happened When Marissa Mayer Tried to Be Steve Jobs. Retrieved December 2023 from https://www.nytimes.com/2014/12/21/magazine/what-happened-when-marissa-mayer-tried-to-be-steve-jobs.html

Nicholas Carlson (January 3, 2015). Business Insider. The Three Times Marissa Mayer Refused To Fire Thousands Of Yahoo Employees. Retrieved December 2023 from https://www.businessinsider.com/marissa-mayer-refused-to-fire-thousands-of-yahoo-employees-2015-1

Nicholas Carlson (July 23, 2011). Business Insider. Agency Execs Say Bartz Massively Understated Yahoo's Sales Force Problem. Retrieved December 2023 from https://www.businessinsider.com/agency-execs-say-bartz-massively-understated-yahoos-sales-force-problem-2011-7

Oxford Reference. Yin-Yang. Retrieved December 2023 from https://www.oxfor
dreference.com/display/10.1093/oi/authority.20110803125343848

Patricia Sellers (September 8, 2011). Fortune. Carol Bartz exclusive: Yahoo "f—
ed me over". Retrieved December 2023 from https://fortune.com/2011/09/
08/carol-bartz-exclusive-yahoo-f-ed-me-over/

Patrick Thibodeau (September 4, 2015). Computerworld. Older IT pros pushed
aside by younger H-1B workers. H-1B visas go primarily to people who are
under 35, suggesting that the threat of age discrimination may be central
to much of the hostility surrounding the controversial program. Retrieved
December 2023 from https://www.computerworld.com/article/2978948/
older-it-pros-pushed-aside-by-younger-h-1b-workers.html

Paul R. La Monica (June 13, 2017). CNN Money. Marissa Mayer leaves Yahoo
with nearly $260 million. Retrieved December 2023 from https://money.
cnn.com/2017/06/13/investing/yahoo-marissa-mayer-severance-stock-
verizon/index.html

Peter Cohan (July 13, 2012). Forbes. Why Stack Ranking Worked Better at GE
Than Microsoft. Retrieved December 2023 from https://www.forbes.com/
sites/petercohan/2012/07/13/why-stack-ranking-worked-better-at-ge-
than-microsoft

Phys.org (June 20, 2011). Facebook to pass Yahoo! in display ad revenue.
Retrieved December 2023 from https://phys.org/news/2011-06-facebook-
yahoo-ad-revenue.html

Preston Gralla (July 5, 2012). Computerworld. Microsoft's downfall:
Bureaucracy, over-reliance on Windows, and poor HR management, says
Vanity Fair. Retrieved December 2023 from https://www.computerworld.
com/article/2597464/microsoft-s-downfall--bureacuracy--over-reliance-
on-windows--and-poor-hr-managemen.html

Rana Foroohar (July 30, 2012). TIME. She's Feeling Lucky. Why mother-to-be
Marissa Mayer is a smart pick to reinvent a laboring Yahoo. Retrieved
December 2023 from https://content.time.com/time/subscriber/arti
cle/0,33009,2119897,00.html

Redwood National and State Parks California. National Park Service. About the
Trees. Retrieved December 2023 from https://www.nps.gov/redw/learn/
nature/about-the-trees.htm

Reuters (September 7, 2011). Yahoo CEO Bartz fired over the phone, rocky run
ends. Retrieved December 2023 from https://www.reuters.com/article/us-
yahoo-ceo/yahoo-ceo-bartz-fired-over-the-phone-rocky-run-ends-idUS
TRE7857R320110907

Rip Empson (March 25, 2012). TechCrunch. Proxy Fight Looms As Yahoo
Appoints Three New Board Members. Retrieved December 2023 from
https://techcrunch.com/2012/03/25/yahoo-three-new-board-members

RoadsideAmerica.com, Field Review. Immortal Tree. Retrieved December 2023 from https://www.roadsideamerica.com/story/21677

Selena Larson (October 4, 2017). CNN Money. Every single Yahoo account was hacked - 3 billion in all. Retrieved December 2023 from https://money.cnn.com/2017/10/03/technology/business/yahoo-breach-3-billion-accounts

Social Security Administration. Starting Your Retirement Benefits Early. Retrieved December 2023 from https://www.ssa.gov/benefits/retirement/planner/agereduction.html

The Associated Press via Yahoo! News (April 4, 2012). Job cuts at Yahoo: 6 rounds of layoffs in 4 years. Retrieved December 2023 from https://www.yahoo.com/news/job-cuts-yahoo-6-rounds-181252551.html

Thomas H. Davenport and DJ Patil (October 2012). Harvard Business Review. Data Scientist: The Sexiest Job of the 21st Century. Meet the people who can coax treasure out of messy, unstructured data. Retrieved December 2023 from https://hbr.org/2012/10/data-scientist-the-sexiest-job-of-the-21st-century

Vanity Fair (July 3, 2012). Microsoft's Downfall: Inside the Executive E-mails and Cannibalistic Culture That Felled a Tech Giant. Retrieved December 2023 from https://www.vanityfair.com/news/2012/07/microsoft-downfall-emails-steve-ballmer

Verne G. Kopytoff, Claire Cain Miller (September 6, 2011). New York Times. Yahoo Board Fires Chief Executive. Retrieved December 2023 from https://www.nytimes.com/2011/09/07/technology/carol-bartz-yahoos-chief-executive-is-fired.html

Vindu Goel (February 1, 2016). New York Times. A Yahoo Employee-Ranking System Favored by Marissa Mayer Is Challenged in Court. Retrieved December 2023 from https://www.nytimes.com/2016/02/02/technology/yahoo-employee-ranking-system-lawsuit.html

Wikipedia. Avenue of the Giants. Retrieved December 2023 from https://en.wikipedia.org/wiki/Avenue_of_the_Giants#Immortal_Tree

Wikipedia. Forks Over Knives. Retrieved December 2023 from https://en.wikipedia.org/wiki/Forks_Over_Knives

Wikipedia. Gary Numan. Retrieved December 2023 from https://en.wikipedia.org/wiki/Gary_Numan#Personal_life

Wikipedia. H-1B visa. Retrieved December 2023 from https://en.wikipedia.org/wiki/H-1B_visa#Criticism

Wikipedia. Ram Dass. Retrieved December 2023 from https://en.wikipedia.org/wiki/Ram_Dass

Wikipedia. Sequoia sempervirens. Retrieved December 2023 from https://en.wikipedia.org/wiki/Sequoia_sempervirens

Wikipedia. Vulcan (Star Trek). Retrieved December 2023 from https://en.wikipedia.org/wiki/Vulcan_(Star_Trek)#Mind_melds

Zameena Mejia (May 31, 2017). CNBC. Why Marissa Mayer is the 'least likable'

CEO in tech. Retrieved December 2023 from https://www.cnbc.com/2017/ 05/31/why-yahoo-ceo-marissa-mayer-is-the-least-likable-ceo-in- tech.html

3. RESPONSIBILITY

American Oceans. How Far Does the Arctic Tern Migrate? Retrieved December 2023 from https://www.americanoceans.org/facts/how-far-arctic-tern- migrate/

Ben Popper (November 11, 2016). The Verge. Why GoPro's Karma drone came crashing down. The dream of an American-made drone may be dead. Retrieved December 2023 from https://www.theverge.com/2016/11/11/ 13597902/gopro-karma-drone-recall-crash-battery-fail

Brent Rose (September 19, 2016). WIRED. GoPro's Karma Drone and New Cameras Look Mighty Hot. Retrieved December 2023 from https://www. wired.com/2016/09/gopros-karma-drone-new-cameras-look-mighty-hot/

California's Great America. Drop Tower. Extreme Fear by the Numbers. Retrieved December 2023 from https://www.cagreatamerica.com/rides- experiences/drop-tower

Cambridge Dictionary. Flighty. Retrieved December 2023 from https://dictio nary.cambridge.org/us/dictionary/english/flighty

David Hellier (January 15, 2016). The Guardian. From GoPro to oh no! Investors reeling from stock price plunge. Shareholders have been left unimpressed by the fall in price from $94 to $12 and are reaching for their lawyers. Retrieved December 2023 from https://www.theguardian.com/business/ 2016/jan/15/gopro-investors-reel-after-stock-price-plunge

Evan Niu (November 30, 2016). The Motley Fool. As Expected, GoPro Abandons Its Entertainment Business. Retrieved December 2023 from https://www.fool.com/investing/2016/11/30/as-expected-gopro-aban dons-its-entertainment-busin.aspx

GoPro (October 28, 2014). YouTube. GoPro: Descent Into the Lava of Marum in 4K. Retrieved December 2023 from https://www.youtube.com/watch?v= toxDDERtvOY

GoPro (September 29, 2014). YouTube. GoPro HERO4: The Adventure of Life in 4K. Retrieved December 2023 from https://www.youtube.com/watch?v= wTcNtgA6gHs

GoPro News (September 19, 2016). The Launch: GoPro Unveils HERO5 and Karma. Retrieved December 2023 from https://gopro.com/en/us/ news/The-Launch-GoPro-Unveils-HERO5-and-Karma

GoPro Press Releases and Media Alerts (November 8, 2016). GoPro Announces Karma Recall and Refund Program. Retrieved December 2023 from https:// investor.gopro.com/press-releases/press-release-details/2016/GoPro-

Announces-Karma-Recall-and-Refund-Program/default.aspx

GoPro, Inc. Proxy Statement for 2016 Annual Meeting of Stockholders (April 22, 2016). United States Securities and Exchange Commission. Retrieved December 2023 from https://www.sec.gov/Archives/edgar/data/1500435/000150043516000082/gpro2016proxystatement.htm

Joshua Goldman (December 4, 2015). CNET. GoPro cuts Hero4 Session camera price again after sales fail to take off. The waterproof cube-shaped camera is the company's smallest, but it looks like it'll take an equally petite price to spark sales. Retrieved December 2023 from https://www.cnet.com/tech/computing/gopro-cuts-hero4-session-price-to-200-160-and-au300/

Krysia Lenzo (March 1, 2016). CNBC. Woodman: This is the biggest year ever for GoPro. Retrieved December 2023 from https://www.cnbc.com/2016/03/01/woodman-this-is-the-biggest-year-ever-for-gopro.html

Matt Egan (April 17, 2015). CNN Money. America's highest paid CEO earns $285 million. Apparently GoPro's "extreme" culture even applies to how much money it pays its founder and CEO. Retrieved December 2023 from https://money.cnn.com/2015/04/17/investing/gopro-founder-nick-woodman-highest-paid-ceo-2014/index.html

National Oceanic and Atmospheric Administration. Science on a Sphere. Retrieved December 2023 from https://sos.noaa.gov/

Noel Randewich (December 31, 2015). Reuters. Wall Street suffers feeble end to turbulent 2015. Retrieved December 2023 from https://www.reuters.com/article/us-usa-stocks/wall-street-suffers-feeble-end-to-turbulent-2015-idUSKBN0UE0TS20151231

Patti Domm, Antonio José Vielma (December 30, 2016). CNBC. Stocks close out 2016 with double-digit gains after third day of losses. Retrieved December 2023 from https://www.cnbc.com/2016/12/30/the-dow-could-ring-out-2016-with-a-near-14-percent-gain.html

Paul R. La Monica (December 15, 2016). CNN Money. GoPro is a no go. Stock hits all-time low. Retrieved December 2023 from https://money.cnn.com/2016/12/15/investing/gorpro-stock-all-time-low/

Richard Lawler (November 3, 2016). Engadget. GoPro's production issues cut into its sales and stock price. The company has high hopes for the Karma and Hero5, but it could be 2017 before it's profitable again. Retrieved December 2023 from https://www.engadget.com/2016-11-03-gopros-production-issues-cut-into-its-sales-and-stock-price.html

Sara Ashley O'Brien (January 13,2016). CNN Money. GoPro to cut 7% of workforce; shares plunge 25%. Retrieved December 2023 from https://money.cnn.com/2016/01/13/investing/gopro-layoffs-weak-sales/index.html

Selina Wang (March 11, 2017). Toronto Star. Can COO CJ Prober stop the flow of GoPro's record lows? CJ Prober pledges to hold the line on costs, make the cameras easier to use and chase international growth. Retrieved

December 2023 from https://www.thestar.com/business/can-coo-cj-prober-stop-the-flow-of-gopro-s-record-lows/article_03d52dcc-cb50-5fc5-b7ab-55670a289d3b.html

Stanford Law School, Securities Class Action Clearinghouse. Case Summary. GoPro, Inc. Securities Litigation. Filing Date: January 13, 2016. Retrieved December 2023 from https://securities.stanford.edu/filings-case.html?id=105735

Timothy Green (October 10, 2018). The Motley Fool. Why GoPro Stock Crashed 52% in 2016. Last year featured big revenue declines, significant losses, and a major product failure. 2017 should be better -- if only because it can't get any worse. Retrieved December 2023 from https://www.fool.com/invest ing/2017/01/03/why-gopro-stock-crashed-52-in-2016.aspx

Wikipedia. 2016 United States presidential election. Retrieved December 2023 from https://en.wikipedia.org/wiki/2016_United_States_presidential_elec tion

Wikipedia. GoPro. Retrieved December 2023 from https://en.wikipedia.org/wiki/GoPro#Product_lines

Wikipedia. Nasdaq Composite. Retrieved December 2023 from https://en.wiki pedia.org/wiki/Nasdaq_Composite#Returns_by_year

4. LISTENING

@biomimicryinstitute (April 19, 2017). Instagram. Nature's 10 Unifying Patterns. Retrieved December 2023 from https://www.instagram.com/p/BTFF_dxllcb

Aaron Flores (March 2, 2018). National Eating Disorders Association. What Does Intuitive Eating Mean? Retrieved December 2023 from https://www.nationaleatingdisorders.org/what-does-intuitive-eating-mean

Angela Amico, Margo Wootan, Michael Jacobson, Cindy Leung, Walter Willett. The Demise of Artificial Trans Fat: A History of a Public Health Achievement. Milbank Q. 2021 Sep;99(3):746-770. doi: 10.1111/1468-0009.12515. Epub 2021 Aug 3. PMID: 34342900; PMCID: PMC8452362. Retrieved December 2023 from https://www.ncbi.nlm.nih.gov/pmc/arti cles/PMC8452362/

Biomimicry Institute. Nature's Unifying Patterns. Learning from nature's over-arching design lessons. Retrieved December 2023 from https://toolbox.biomimicry.org/core-concepts/natures-unifying-patterns/

Biomimicry Institute. What is biomimicry? Retrieved December 2023 from https://biomimicry.org/what-is-biomimicry/

Carnegie Museum of Natural History. Biomimicry is Real World Inspiration. Retrieved December 2023 from https://carnegiemnh.org/biomimicry-is-real-world-inspiration/

Cleveland Clinic (August 13, 2021). Heimlich Maneuver. Retrieved December 2023 from https://my.clevelandclinic.org/health/treatments/21675-heimlich-maneuver

Heather Plett (March 11, 2015). What it means to "hold space" for people, plus eight tips on how to do it well. Retrieved December 2023 from https://heatherplett.com/2015/03/hold-space/

Institute of Medicine (US) Committee on Examination of Front-of-Package Nutrition Rating Systems and Symbols; Wartella EA, Lichtenstein AH, Boon CS, editors. Front-of-Package Nutrition Rating Systems and Symbols: Phase I Report. Washington (DC): National Academies Press (US); 2010. 2, History of Nutrition Labeling. Retrieved December 2023 from https://www.ncbi.nlm.nih.gov/books/NBK209859/

K. Michael Cummings, Robert N. Proctor; The Changing Public Image of Smoking in the United States: 1964–2014. Cancer Epidemiol Biomarkers Prev 1 January 2014; 23 (1): 32–36. Retrieved December 2023 from https://aacrjournals.org/cebp/article/23/1/32/158084/The-Changing-Public-Image-of-Smoking-in-the-United

Karen Jennings Evans, Julia Y. Trankiem (July 26, 2018). Hunton Andrews Kurth. California Clarifies Its Law Banning Inquiries into Applicants' Salary History. Retrieved December 2023 from https://www.huntonlaborblog.com/2018/07/articles/california-developments/california-clarifies-law-banning-inquiries-applicants-salary-history/

Laura Italiano (July 28, 2018). New York Post. Homeless man hands out resumes, gets hundreds of job offers. Retrieved December 2023 from https://nypost.com/2018/07/28/homeless-man-hands-out-resumes-gets-hundreds-of-job-offers/

Laurel J. Felt & Michael B. Robb (2016). Technology addiction: Concern, controversy, and finding balance. San Francisco, CA: Common Sense Media. Retrieved December 2023 from https://www.commonsensemedia.org/sites/default/files/research/report/2016_csm_technology_addiction_executive_summary.pdf

Pedro Nicolaci Da Costa (March 2019). International Monetary Fund. Tech Talent Scramble. Global competition for a limited pool of technology workers is heating up. Retrieved December 2023 from https://www.imf.org/en/Publications/fandd/issues/2019/03/global-competition-for-technology-workers-costa

Psychology Today (June 2, 2022). Somatic Therapy. Retrieved December 2023 from https://www.psychologytoday.com/us/therapy-types/somatic-therapy

Robert D. McFadden (December 7, 2016). New York Times. Dr. Henry J. Heimlich, Famous for Antichoking Technique, Dies at 96. Retrieved December 2023 from https://www.nytimes.com/2016/12/17/us/dr-henry-j-heimlich-famous-for-antichoking-technique-dies-at-96.html

Sarah Epstein (May 25, 2023). Psychology Today. What Does It Mean to Hold Space? Learn the art of "holding space" for people in your life. Retrieved December 2023 from https://www.psychologytoday.com/us/blog/between-the-generations/202305/what-does-it-mean-to-hold-space

Sheelah Kolhatkar (November 13, 2017). The New Yorker. The Tech Industry's Gender-Discrimination Problem. The dramatic imbalance in pay and power has created the conditions for abuse. More and more, women are pushing for change. Retrieved December 2023 from https://www.newyorker.com/magazine/2017/11/20/the-tech-industrys-gender-discrimination-problem

Sherrie Bourg Carter (October 20, 2012). Psychology Today. Emotions Are Contagious—Choose Your Company Wisely. Second-hand emotions: the good, the bad and the ugly. Retrieved December 2023 from https://www.psychologytoday.com/us/blog/high-octane-women/201210/emotions-are-contagious-choose-your-company-wisely

Ugonma Nwankwo, Michael Pisa (March 8, 2021). Center for Global Development. Why the World Needs More Women Data Scientists. Retrieved December 2023 from https://www.cgdev.org/blog/why-world-needs-more-women-data-scientists

Wildsight. Seasonal Sit Spots. Retrieved December 2023 from https://wildsight.ca/education-resources/sit-spots/

5. TRANSFORMATION

Alphabet Inc. Form 10-K For the Fiscal Year Ended December 31, 2019. United States Securities and Exchange Commission. Retrieved December 2023 from https://www.sec.gov/ix?doc=/Archives/edgar/data/0001652044/000165204420000008/goog10-k2019.htm

Arlin Cuncic (November 9, 2023). Verywell Mind. 12 Signs of a Vulnerable Narcissist. Retrieved December 2023 from https://www.verywellmind.com/signs-of-a-vulnerable-narcissist-7369901

Biology Online. Dictionary. Kleptoparasitism. Retrieved December 2023 from https://www.biologyonline.com/dictionary/kleptoparasitism

California Department of Forestry and Fire Protection (May 15, 2019). News Release. CAL FIRE Investigators Determine Cause of the Camp Fire. Retrieved December 2023 from https://web.archive.org/web/20210128061532/https://www.fire.ca.gov/media/5121/campfire_cause.pdf

California Department of Forestry and Fire Protection. Incidents. Woodward Fire. Retrieved December 2023 from https://www.fire.ca.gov/incidents/2020/8/18/woodward-fire/

Courtney Connley (September 20, 2018). CNBC. A new report highlights

Silicon Valley's stunning gender equity gap. Retrieved December 2023 from https://www.cnbc.com/2018/09/19/in-silicon-valley-women-face-an-equity-gap-that-is-far-larger-than-the-pay-gap.html

Daisuke Wakabayashi (May 28, 2019). New York Times. Google's Shadow Work Force: Temps Who Outnumber Full-Time Employees. Retrieved December 2023 from https://www.nytimes.com/2019/05/28/technology/google-temp-workers.html

Emily Wilson (June 18, 2003). Half Moon Bay Review. Honor camp in La Honda set to close. Retrieved December 2023 from https://www.hmbreview.com/honor-camp-in-la-honda-set-to-close/article_b30ce3bc-7c6e-50a1-8778-16e3aec4049c.html

Employer's Resource Council (November 5, 2013). 20 Subtle Signs of Bullying at Work. Retrieved December 2023 from https://yourerc.com/blog/20-subtle-signs-of-workplace-bullying/

Harmeet Kaur (October 24, 2019). CNN. Why Californians are furious at the utility company PG&E. Retrieved December 2023 from https://www.cnn.com/2019/10/10/us/pge-power-outages-public-outrage-trnd/index.html

Insight Vacations (February 24, 2023). Pretty in pink: The story behind why Jaipur is so famously known as 'The Pink City'. Retrieved December 2023 from https://www.insightvacations.com/blog/story-jaipur-pink-city/

Jodi Clarke (December 5, 2023). Verywell Mind. How to Recognize a Covert Narcissist. Retrieved December 2023 from https://www.verywellmind.com/understanding-the-covert-narcissist-4584587#toc-how-to-deal-with-a-covert-narcissist

Julia Carrie Wong (June 25, 2019). The Guardian. 'A white-collar sweatshop': Google Assistant contractors allege wage theft. Retrieved December 2023 from   https://www.theguardian.com/technology/2019/may/28/a-white-collar-sweatshop-google-assistant-contractors-allege-wage-theft

Ibid.

Kari Paul (September 9, 2020). The Guardian. 'Good morning, hell': Californians awake to apocalyptic skies as wildfires rage. Orange-hued skies are due to light being filtered through smoke from the state's worst fire season on record. Retrieved December 2023 from https://www.theguardian.com/us-news/2020/sep/09/orange-sky-california-fires-smoke-san-francisco

Kendra Cherry (October 14, 2022). Verywell Mind. How to Deal With a Narcissist. Tips for Living With a Narcissist. Retrieved December 2023 from https://www.verywellmind.com/living-with-a-narcissist-tips-for-how-to-cope-5211902

Mark Noack (September 13, 2012). Half Moon Bay Review. La Honda Jail could unlock new campsite. Former honor camp might be transformed. Retrieved December 2023 from https://www.hmbreview.com/news/la-honda-jail-could-unlock-new-campsite/article_34180c5a-fdcb-11e1-8ea3-0019bb2963f4.html

Markus MacGill, Rachel Ann Tee-Melegrito (February 15, 2023). Medical News Today. What is psychosis? Retrieved December 2023 from https://www.medicalnewstoday.com/articles/248159

MasterClass (October 23, 2022). Plato's Allegory of the Cave Explained. Retrieved December 2023 from https://www.masterclass.com/articles/allegory-of-the-cave-explainede

Matt Dupuy (June 11, 2021). The Register. Women techs fume, offer crowd-sourced fixes as Michelle Obama's online keynote crashes. 'Unforeseen server conditions' blamed. Retrieved December 2023 from https://www.theregister.com/2021/06/11/women_tech_obama/

Pew Research Center (March 30, 2021). Women remain underrepresented in physical sciences, computing and engineering jobs. Retrieved December 2023 from https://www.pewresearch.org/social-trends/2021/04/01/stem-jobs-see-uneven-progress-in-increasing-gender-racial-and-ethnic-diversity/ps_2021-04-01_diversity-in-stem_00-03-png/

Psycom (November 2, 2021). Gaslighting: What Is It and Why Do People Do It? Retrieved December 2023 from https://www.psycom.net/gaslighting-what-is-it

Rani Molla (May 31, 2019). Vox. How much Google contractors say they get paid compared to full-time employees. We use Glassdoor data to take a look at the opaque world of Google contractor treatment and pay. Retrieved December 2023 from https://www.vox.com/recode/2019/5/31/18644866/google-contractors-pay-ratings-glassdoor

Ruth Umoh (June 29, 2017). CNBC. Steve Jobs and Albert Einstein both attributed their extraordinary success to this personality trait. Retrieved December 2023 from https://www.cnbc.com/2017/06/29/steve-jobs-and-albert-einstein-both-attributed-their-extraordinary-success-to-this-personality-trait.html

Sebastian Moss (December 2, 2021). DatacenterDynamics. Underpaid and overworked: Behind the scenes with Google's data center contractors. Contractors and Google employees speak out against a broken culture. Retrieved December 2023 from https://www.datacenterdynamics.com/en/analysis/underpaid-and-overworked-behind-the-scenes-with-googles-data-center-contractors/

Sherri Gordon (November 21, 2023). Verywell Mind. Is Someone Gaslighting You? Learn the Warning Signs. Retrieved December 2023 from https://www.verywellmind.com/is-someone-gaslighting-you-4147470

Silvi Saxena (May 6, 2023). Choosing Therapy. Vulnerable Narcissists: 11 Signs & How to Deal With One. Retrieved December 2023 from https://www.choosingtherapy.com/vulnerable-narcissist/

Susan Fishman (August 3, 2023). PsychCentral. 5 Ways to Identify a Vulnerable Narcissist. Retrieved December 2023 from https://psychcentral.com/disor ders/the-secret-facade-of-the-vulnerable-narcissist#dealing-with-vulnera ble-narcissists

The Allen Ginsberg Project (June 14, 2014). First Party At Ken Kesey's With Hell's Angels. Retrieved December 2023 from https://allenginsberg.org/ 2014/06/first-party-at-ken-keseys-with-hells-angels/

The Associated Press via TODAY (January 20, 2004). Ken Kesey's journal from jail published. Words, drawings meld in manuscript. Retrieved December 2023 from https://www.today.com/popculture/ken-kesey-s-journal-jail-published-wbna3949414

Wikipedia. 2019 California power shutoffs. Retrieved December 2023 from https://en.wikipedia.org/wiki/2019_California_power_shutoffs

Wikipedia. Adjustment disorder. Retrieved December 2023 from https://en. wikipedia.org/wiki/Adjustment_disorder

Wikipedia. Adjustment disorder. Retrieved December 2023 from https://en. wikipedia.org/wiki/Adjustment_disorder#In_relation_to_the_COVID-19_pandemic

Wikipedia. California Consumer Privacy Act. Retrieved December 2023 from https://en.wikipedia.org/wiki/California_Consumer_Privacy_Act

Wikipedia. CZU Lightning Complex fires. Retrieved December 2023 from https://en.wikipedia.org/wiki/CZU_Lightning_Complex_fires

Wikipedia. General Data Protection Regulation. Retrieved December 2023 from https://en.wikipedia.org/wiki/General_Data_Protection_Regulation

Wikipedia. Ken Kesey. Retrieved December 2023 from https://en.wikipedia. org/wiki/Ken_Kesey#One_Flew_Over_the_Cuckoo's_Nest

Wikipedia. One Flew Over the Cuckoo's Nest (novel). Retrieved December 2023 from https://en.wikipedia.org/wiki/One_Flew_Over_the_Cuckoo% 27s_Nest_(novel)

Wikipedia. Pacific Gas and Electric Company. Retrieved December 2023 from https://en.wikipedia.org/wiki/Pacific_Gas_and_Electric_Com pany#Wildfires

6. CONCLUSIONS

Alphabet Inc. Form 10-Q For the Quarterly Period Ended September 30, 2023. United States Securities and Exchange Commission. Retrieved December 2023 from https://www.sec.gov/ix?doc=/Archives/edgar/data/1652044/ 000165204423000094/goog-20230930.htm

Alphabet Union, CWA Local 9009. About Us. Google's Motto used to be "Don't Be Evil" – we are working to make sure they live up to that AND more. Retrieved December 2023 from https://www.alphabetworkersunion.org/

about-us

Alphabet Union, CWA Local 9009. Home Page. We are a fighting union. Our union of 1400+ is building power for all Alphabet workers. Retrieved December 2023 from https://www.alphabetworkersunion.org

Apple (December 11, 2023). Apple launches Journal, a new app to reflect on everyday moments and life's special events. Retrieved December 2023 from https://www.apple.com/newsroom/2023/12/apple-launches-journal-app-a-new-app-for-reflecting-on-everyday-moments/

Brian Fung (October 2, 2023). CNN. Microsoft CEO warns of 'nightmare' future for AI if Google's search dominance continues. Retrieved December 2023 from   https://www.cnn.com/2023/10/02/tech/microsoft-warning-google-search-monopoly/index.html

CBS News Bay Area (October 24, 2023). California among states suing Meta for harming mental health of young people. Retrieved December 2023 from https://www.cbsnews.com/sanfrancisco/news/california-among-33-states-suing-meta-young-people-mental-health-facebook-instagram/

CloudChef. Serve Michelin-like dishes, with untrained staff. Retrieved December 2023 from https://www.cloudchef.co/platform

Lauren Saria (March 23, 2023). Eater San Francisco. A.I.: It's What's for Dinner. Silicon Valley startup CloudChef says its artificially intelligent software could be the future for restaurants. Retrieved December 2023 from https://sf.eater.com/2023/3/23/23648952/cloudchef-software-restaurnats-ai

Lisa Richwine, Dawn Chmielewski and Danielle Broadway (November 9, 2023). Reuters. Hollywood actors reach tentative deal with studios to end strike. Retrieved December 2023 from https://www.reuters.com/business/media-telecom/striking-actors-reach-tentative-agreement-with-hollywood-studios-end-strike-2023-11-09/

Steve Lohr (January 10, 2021). New York Times. He Created the Web. Now He's Out to Remake the Digital World. Tim Berners-Lee wants to put people in control of their personal data. He has technology and a start-up pursuing that goal. Can he succeed? Retrieved December 2023 from https://www.nytimes.com/2021/01/10/technology/tim-berners-lee-privacy-internet.html

The White House (October 30, 2023). FACT SHEET: President Biden Issues Executive Order on Safe, Secure, and Trustworthy Artificial Intelligence. Retrieved December 2023 from https://www.whitehouse.gov/briefing-room/statements-releases/2023/10/30/fact-sheet-president-biden-issues-executive-order-on-safe-secure-and-trustworthy-artificial-intelligence

EPILOGUE

Olympics (October 8, 2023). Artistic Gymnastics World Championships 2023: Simone Biles claims two more golds on final day of competition. The USA gymnast now has 23 career wins at the global meet and 30 overall medals. Retrieved December 2023 from https://olympics.com/en/news/artistic-gymnastics-world-championships-2023-apparatus-finals-simone-biles-two-golds-final-day

OlympicTalk (October 8, 2023). NBC Sports. Simone Biles closes gymnastics worlds with two more gold medals. Retrieved December 2023 from https://www.nbcsports.com/olympics/news/simone-biles-gymnastics-world-championships-2023-medals

Sophie Lewis (July 30, 2021). CBS News. Simone Biles opens up about withdrawal from Olympic competitions: "I don't think you realize how dangerous this is". Retrieved December 2023 from https://www.cbsnews.com/news/simone-biles-olympics-gymnastics-withdrawal-twisties/

NOTES

1. AWARENESS

1. CERN. World Wide Web. Retrieved December 2023 from https://info.cern. ch/hypertext/WWW/TheProject.html
2. *Merriam-Webster Dictionary*. Algorithm. Retrieved December 2023 from https://www.merriam-webster.com/dictionary/algorithm
3. Matthew Gray of the Massachusetts Institute of Technology (1996). Web Growth Summary. Retrieved December 2023 from https://www.mit.edu/people/mkgray/net/web-growth-summary.html
4. CERN. A short history of the Web. Retrieved December 2023 from https://home.cern/science/computing/birth-web/short-history-web
5. *WIRED* (July 19, 2000). Why CNET Bought ZDNet. Retrieved December 2023 from https://wired.com/2000/07/why-cnet-bought-zdnet/amp
6. Seeking Alpha (April 18, 2006). Yahoo! Q1 2006 Earnings Call Transcript. Retrieved December 2023 from https://seekingalpha.com/article/9173-yahoo-q1-2006-earnings-call-transcript
7. Comscore (May 4, 2006). Press Release. 694 Million People Currently Use the Internet Worldwide According To Comscore Networks. Retrieved December 2023 from https://www.comscore.com/Insights/Press-Releases/2006/05/comScore-Launches-World-Metrix
8. Internet Live Stats. Total number of Websites. Retrieved December 2023 from https://www.internetlivestats.com/total-number-of-websites/
9. Comscore (May 4, 2006). Press Release. 694 Million People Currently Use the Internet Worldwide According To Comscore Networks. Retrieved December 2023 from https://www.comscore.com/Insights/Press-Releases/2006/05/comScore-Launches-World-Metrix
10. Mike Hoefflinger (Apr 16, 2017). *Business Insider*. Inside Mark Zuckerberg's controversial decision to turn down Yahoo's $1 billion early offer to buy Facebook. Retrieved December 2023 from https://www.businessinsider.com/why-mark-zuckerberg-turned-down-yahoos-1-billion-offer-to-buy-facebook-in-2006-2017-4
11. Michael Arrington (September 6, 2006). TechCrunch. Facebook Users Revolt, Facebook Replies. Retrieved December 2023 from https://techcrunch.com/2006/09/06/facebook-users-revolt-facebook-replies/
12. Comscore (July 12, 2007). Press Release. 772 Million People Online Worldwide in May. Online Retail and E-Commerce Sites Boosted by Holiday Spending. Retrieved December 2023 from https://www.comscore.com/Insights/Press-Releases/2007/07/Top-Worldwide-Web-Properties

13. Miguel Helft (January 22, 2008). *New York Times*. Hundreds of Layoffs Expected at Yahoo. Retrieved December 2023 from https://www.nytimes.com/2008/01/22/technology/22yahoo.html

14. Comscore (February 5, 2008). Press Release. Media Advisory: Microsoft Bids on Yahoo!. Retrieved December 2023 from https://www.comscore.com/Insights/Press-Releases/2008/02/Microsoft-Bids-on-Yahoo

15. Chris Isidore of CNNMoney.com, Michal Lev-Ram of *Fortune* (February 1, 2008). Microsoft bids $45 billion for Yahoo. Software giant offers $31 a share - a 62% premium - in deal that could reorder online ad market. Microsoft's Ballmer: 'Major milestone.' Retrieved December 2023 from https://money.cnn.com/2008/02/01/technology/microsoft_yahoo/

16. BBC News (March 17, 2008). Microsoft's moves 'threaten net'. Any deal between Yahoo and Microsoft could be "bad for the internet", according to the head of Google. Retrieved December 2023 from http://news.bbc.co.uk/2/hi/technology/7300337.stm

17. Steve Lohr (May 5, 2008). *New York Times*. Microsoft's Failed Yahoo Bid Risks Online Growth. Retrieved December 2023 from https://www.nytimes.com/2008/05/05/technology/05soft.html

18. Stephen Shankland (May 8, 2008). CNET. Google addresses antitrust issue on Yahoo ad deal. Microsoft is concerned an ad deal with Yahoo would extend Google's search-ad dominance. Google execs says people should look at the bigger ad market. Retrieved December 2023 from https://www.cnet.com/culture/google-addresses-antitrust-issue-on-yahoo-ad-deal/

19. Miguel Helft (October 21, 2008). *New York Times*. Yahoo to Cut About 10% of Workers. Retrieved December 2023 from https://www.nytimes.com/2008/10/22/technology/companies/22yahoo.html

20. Wikipedia. Carol Bartz. Retrieved December 2023 from https://en.wikipedia.org/wiki/Carol_Bartz#CEO_of_Yahoo

21. Stephen Shankland (April 21, 2009). CNET. Yahoo plans layoff after profit plunges. Several hundred employees will lose jobs in coming weeks as the online pioneer tries to change course. Retrieved December 2023 from https://www.cnet.com/tech/services-and-software/yahoo-plans-layoff-after-profit-plunges/

22. Reuters (July 30, 2009). Microsoft, Yahoo in Web search partnership. Retrieved December 2023 from https://www.reuters.com/article/uk-microsoft-yahoo-sb/microsoft-yahoo-in-web-search-partnership-idUKTRE56T1A520090730

23. David Goldman (July 29, 2009). CNN Money. Microsoft and Yahoo: Search partners. After a year and a half of dealing, the tech giants reach a 10-year deal to take on Google, which holds a 65% market share in online search. Retrieved December 2023 from https://money.cnn.com/2009/07/29/technology/microsoft_yahoo/

24. Doug Gross (November 17, 2009). CNN. Dictionary word of the year: 'Unfriend.' Retrieved December 2023 from https://www.cnn.com/2009/TECH/11/17/unfriend.word/index.html

25. Google Official Blog (July 25, 2008). We knew the web was big... Retrieved December 2023 from https://googleblog.blogspot.com/2008/07/we-knew-web-was-big.html

2. AWAKENING

1. *Oxford Reference.* Yin-Yang. Retrieved December 2023 from https://www.oxfordreference.com/display/10.1093/oi/authority.20110803125343848

2. Jon Hamilton (April 7, 2011). NPR, Morning Edition. In Japan, Shaken Soil Turned Soft After Quake. Retrieved December 2023 from https://www.npr.org/2011/04/07/135181474/in-japan-shaken-soil-turned-soft-after-quake

3. Wikipedia. Ram Dass. Retrieved December 2023 from https://en.wikipedia.org/wiki/Ram_Dass

4. Patricia Sellers (September 8, 2011). *Fortune.* Carol Bartz exclusive: Yahoo "f—ed me over". Retrieved December 2023 from https://fortune.com/2011/09/08/carol-bartz-exclusive-yahoo-f-ed-me-over/

5. Julianne Pepitone (February 14, 2012). CNN Money. Activist shareholder Loeb launches Yahoo proxy fight. Retrieved December 2023 from https://money.cnn.com/2012/02/14/technology/yahoo_proxy/index.htm

6. Rip Empson (March 25, 2012). TechCrunch. Proxy Fight Looms As Yahoo Appoints Three New Board Members. Retrieved December 2023 from https://techcrunch.com/2012/03/25/yahoo-three-new-board-members

7. Jessica Guynn (April 5, 2012). *Los Angeles Times.* Yahoo announces 2,000 layoffs as new CEO seeks turnaround. Retrieved December 2023 from https://www.latimes.com/business/la-xpm-2012-apr-05-la-fi-yahoo-layoffs-20120405-story.html

8. *Business Insider* via *Financial Post* (December 21, 2012). Yahoo employees don't approve of Marissa Mayer as much as they used to. Marissa Mayer's approval ratings among Yahoo employees have dropped 17% since her first quarter as CEO. Retrieved December 2023 from https://financialpost.com/business-insider/yahoo-employees-dont-approve-of-marissa-mayer-as-much-as-they-used-to

9. Nicholas Carlson (January 3, 2015). *Business Insider.* The Three Times Marissa Mayer Refused To Fire Thousands Of Yahoo Employees. Retrieved December 2023 from https://www.businessinsider.com/marissa-mayer-refused-to-fire-thousands-of-yahoo-employees-2015-1

10. *Vanity Fair* (July 3, 2012). Microsoft's Downfall: Inside the Executive E-mails and Cannibalistic Culture That Felled a Tech Giant. Retrieved December 2023 from https://www.vanityfair.com/news/2012/07/microsoft-downfall-emails-steve-ballmer

11. Nicholas Carlson (December 17, 2014). *New York Times*. What Happened When Marissa Mayer Tried to Be Steve Jobs. Retrieved December 2023 from https://www.nytimes.com/2014/12/21/magazine/what-happened-when-marissa-mayer-tried-to-be-steve-jobs.html

3. RESPONSIBILITY

1. David Hellier (January 15, 2016). *The Guardian*. From GoPro to oh no! Investors reeling from stock price plunge. Shareholders have been left unimpressed by the fall in price from $94 to $12 and are reaching for their lawyers. Retrieved December 2023 from https://www.theguardian.com/business/2016/jan/15/gopro-investors-reel-after-stock-price-plunge

2. Wikipedia. Nasdaq Composite. Retrieved December 2023 from https://en.wikipedia.org/wiki/Nasdaq_Composite#Returns_by_year. Noel Randewich (December 31, 2015). Reuters. Wall Street suffers feeble end to turbulent 2015. Retrieved December 2023 from https://www.reuters.com/article/us-usa-stocks/wall-street-suffers-feeble-end-to-turbulent-2015-idUSKBN0UE0TS20151231

3. Sara Ashley O'Brien (January 13,2016). CNN Money. GoPro to cut 7% of workforce; shares plunge 25%. Retrieved December 2023 from https://money.cnn.com/2016/01/13/investing/gopro-layoffs-weak-sales/index.html

4. Krysia Lenzo (March 1, 2016). CNBC. Woodman: This is the biggest year ever for GoPro. Retrieved December 2023 from https://www.cnbc.com/2016/03/01/woodman-this-is-the-biggest-year-ever-for-gopro.html

5. GoPro, Inc. Proxy Statement for 2016 Annual Meeting of Stockholders (April 22, 2016). United States Securities and Exchange Commission. Retrieved December 2023 from https://www.sec.gov/Archives/edgar/data/1500435/000150043516000082/gpro2016proxystatement.htm

6. *Cambridge Dictionary*. Meaning of flighty in English. Retrieved December 2023 from https://dictionary.cambridge.org/us/dictionary/english/flighty

7. Stanford Law School, Securities Class Action Clearinghouse. Case Summary. GoPro, Inc. Securities Litigation. Filing Date: November 16, 2016. Retrieved December 2023 from https://securities.stanford.edu/filings-case.html?id=105947

8. Evan Niu (November 30, 2016). The Motley Fool. As Expected, GoPro Abandons Its Entertainment Business. Retrieved December 2023 from https://www.fool.com/investing/2016/11/30/as-expected-gopro-abandons-its-entertainment-busin.aspx. Selina Wang (March 11, 2017). *Toronto Star*. Can COO CJ Prober stop the flow of GoPro's record lows? CJ Prober pledges to hold the line on costs, make the cameras easier to use and chase international growth. Retrieved December 2023 from https://www.thestar.com/business/can-coo-cj-prober-stop-the-flow-of-gopros-record-lows/article_03d52dcc-cb50-5fc5-b7ab-55670a289d3b.html

9. Timothy Green (October 10, 2018). The Motley Fool. Why GoPro Stock Crashed 52% in 2016. Last year featured big revenue declines, significant losses, and a major product failure. 2017 should be better -- if only because it can't get any worse. Retrieved December 2023 from https://www.fool.com/investing/2017/01/03/why-gopro-stock-crashed-52-in-2016.aspx

10. Patti Domm, Antonio José Vielma (December 30, 2016). CNBC. Stocks close out 2016 with double-digit gains after third day of losses. Retrieved December 2023 from https://www.cnbc.com/2016/12/30/the-dow-could-ring-out-2016-with-a-near-14-percent-gain.html

11. Paul R. La Monica (December 15, 2016). CNN Money. GoPro is a no go. Stock hits all-time low. Retrieved December 2023 from https://money.cnn.com/2016/12/15/investing/gorpro-stock-all-time-low/

4. LISTENING

1. Wildsight. Seasonal Sit Spots. Retrieved December 2023 from https://wildsight.ca/education-resources/sit-spots/

2. Sarah Epstein (May 25, 2023). *Psychology Today*. What Does It Mean to Hold Space? Learn the art of "holding space" for people in your life. Retrieved December 2023 from https://www.psychologytoday.com/us/blog/between-the-generations/202305/what-does-it-mean-to-hold-space. Heather Plett (March 11, 2015). What it means to "hold space" for people, plus eight tips on how to do it well. Retrieved December 2023 from https://heatherplett.com/2015/03/hold-space/

3. Biomimicry Institute. What is biomimicry? Retrieved December 2023 from https://biomimicry.org/what-is-biomimicry/

4. Biomimicry Institute. Nature's Unifying Patterns. Learning from nature's overarching design lessons. Retrieved December 2023 from https://toolbox.biomimicry.org/core-concepts/natures-unifying-patterns/

5. @biomimicryinstitute (April 19, 2017). Instagram. Nature's 10 Unifying Patterns. Retrieved December 2023 from https://www.instagram.com/p/BTFF_dxllcb

6. Ugonma Nwankwo, Michael Pisa (March 8, 2021). Center for Global Development. Why the World Needs More Women Data Scientists. Retrieved December 2023 from https://www.cgdev.org/blog/why-world-needs-more-women-data-scientists. Sheelah Kolhatkar (November 13, 2017). *The New Yorker*. The Tech Industry's Gender-Discrimination Problem. The dramatic imbalance in pay and power has created the conditions for abuse. More and more, women are pushing for change. Retrieved December 2023 from https://www.newyorker.com/magazine/2017/11/20/the-tech-industrys-gender-discrimination-problem

7. Pedro Nicolaci Da Costa (March 2019). International Monetary Fund. Tech Talent Scramble. Global competition for a limited pool of technology

workers is heating up. Retrieved December 2023 from https://www.imf.org/en/Publications/fandd/issues/2019/03/global-competition-for-technology-workers-costa

8. Angela Amico, Margo Wootan, Michael Jacobson, Cindy Leung, Walter Willett. The Demise of Artificial Trans Fat: A History of a Public Health Achievement. *Milbank Q.* 2021 Sep;99(3):746-770. doi: 10.1111/1468-0009.12515. Epub 2021 Aug 3. PMID: 34342900; PMCID: PMC8452362. Retrieved December 2023 from https://www.ncbi.nlm.nih.gov/pmc/articles/PMC8452362/

9. Aaron Flores (March 2, 2018). National Eating Disorders Association. What Does Intuitive Eating Mean? Retrieved December 2023 from https://www.nationaleatingdisorders.org/what-does-intuitive-eating-mean

10. Robert D. McFadden (December 7, 2016). *New York Times*. Dr. Henry J. Heimlich, Famous for Antichoking Technique, Dies at 96. Retrieved December 2023 from https://www.nytimes.com/2016/12/17/us/dr-henry-j-heimlich-famous-for-antichoking-technique-dies-at-96.html

11. *Psychology Today* (June 2, 2022). Somatic Therapy. Retrieved December 2023 from https://www.psychologytoday.com/us/therapy-types/somatic-therapy

12. Laura Italiano (July 28, 2018). *New York Post*. Homeless man hands out resumes, gets hundreds of job offers. Retrieved December 2023 from https://nypost.com/2018/07/28/homeless-man-hands-out-resumes-gets-hundreds-of-job-offers/

5. TRANSFORMATION

1. Julia Carrie Wong (June 25, 2019). *The Guardian*. 'A white-collar sweatshop': Google Assistant contractors allege wage theft. Retrieved December 2023 from https://www.theguardian.com/technology/2019/may/28/a-white-collar-sweatshop-google-assistant-contractors-allege-wage-theft. Sebastian Moss (December 2, 2021). DatacenterDynamics. Underpaid and overworked: Behind the scenes with Google's data center contractors. Contractors and Google employees speak out against a broken culture. Retrieved December 2023 from https://www.datacenterdynamics.com/en/analysis/underpaid-and-overworked-behind-the-scenes-with-googles-data-center-contractors/. Rani Molla (May 31, 2019). Vox. How much Google contractors say they get paid compared to full-time employees. We use Glassdoor data to take a look at the opaque world of Google contractor treatment and pay. Retrieved December 2023 from https://www.vox.com/recode/2019/5/31/18644866/google-contractors-pay-ratings-glassdoor

2. Julia Carrie Wong (June 25, 2019). *The Guardian*. 'A white-collar sweatshop': Google Assistant contractors allege wage theft. Retrieved

December 2023 from https://www.theguardian.com/technology/2019/may/28/a-white-collar-sweatshop-google-assistant-contractors-allege-wage-theft

3. Wikipedia. Pacific Gas and Electric Company. Retrieved December 2023 from https://en.wikipedia.org/wiki/Pacific_Gas_and_Electric_Company#Wildfires. California Department of Forestry and Fire Protection (May 15, 2019). News Release. CAL FIRE Investigators Determine Cause of the Camp Fire. Retrieved December 2023 from https://web.archive.org/web/20210128061532/https://www.fire.ca.gov/media/5121/campfire_cause.pdf

4. Wikipedia. Adjustment disorder. Retrieved December 2023 from https://en.wikipedia.org/wiki/Adjustment_disorder

5. Wikipedia. Adjustment disorder. Retrieved December 2023 from https://en.wikipedia.org/wiki/Adjustment_disorder#In_relation_to_the_COVID-19_pandemic

6. Biology Online. Dictionary. Kleptoparasitism. Retrieved December 2023 from https://www.biologyonline.com/dictionary/kleptoparasitism

7. Courtney Connley (September 20, 2018). CNBC. A new report highlights Silicon Valley's stunning gender equity gap. Retrieved December 2023 from https://www.cnbc.com/2018/09/19/in-silicon-valley-women-face-an-equity-gap-that-is-far-larger-than-the-pay-gap.html

8. Pew Research Center (March 30, 2021). Women remain underrepresented in physical sciences, computing and engineering jobs. Retrieved December 2023 from https://www.pewresearch.org/social-trends/2021/04/01/stem-jobs-see-uneven-progress-in-increasing-gender-racial-and-ethnic-diversity/ps_2021-04-01_diversity-in-stem_00-03-png/

6. CLOSING

1. CloudChef. Serve Michelin-like dishes, with untrained staff. Retrieved December 2023 from https://www.cloudchef.co/platform. Lauren Saria (March 23, 2023). Eater San Francisco. A.I.: It's What's for Dinner. Silicon Valley startup CloudChef says its artificially intelligent software could be the future for restaurants. Retrieved December 2023 from https://sf.eater.com/2023/3/23/23648952/cloudchef-software-restaurnats-ai

2. Brian Fung (October 2, 2023). CNN. Microsoft CEO warns of 'nightmare' future for AI if Google's search dominance continues. Retrieved December 2023 from https://www.cnn.com/2023/10/02/tech/microsoft-warning-google-search-monopoly/index.html

3. Steve Lohr (January 10, 2021). *New York Times*. He Created the Web. Now He's Out to Remake the Digital World. Tim Berners-Lee wants to put people in control of their personal data. He has technology and a start-up pursuing that goal. Can he succeed? Retrieved December 2023 from https://www.nytimes.com/2021/01/10/technology/tim-berners-lee-privacy-internet.html

4. The White House (October 30, 2023). FACT SHEET: President Biden Issues Executive Order on Safe, Secure, and Trustworthy Artificial Intelligence. Retrieved December 2023 from https://www.whitehouse.gov/brief ing-room/statements-releases/2023/10/30/fact-sheet-president-biden-issues-executive-order-on-safe-secure-and-trustworthy-artificial-intelli gence

5. Alphabet Union, CWA Local 9009. About Us. Google's Motto used to be "Don't Be Evil" – we are working to make sure they live up to that AND more. Retrieved December 2023 from https://www.alphabetworker sunion.org/about-us and Home Page. We are a fighting union. Our union of 1400+ is building power for all Alphabet workers. Retrieved December 2023 from https://www.alphabetworkersunion.org. Alphabet Inc., Form 10-Q For the Quarterly Period Ended September 30, 2023. United States Securities and Exchange Commission. Retrieved December 2023 from https://www.sec.gov/ix?doc=/Archives/edgar/data/1652044/ 000165204423000094/goog-20230930.htm

EPILOGUE

1. Sophie Lewis (July 30, 2021). CBS News. Simone Biles opens up about withdrawal from Olympic competitions: "I don't think you realize how dangerous this is". Retrieved December 2023 from https://www.cbsnews. com/news/simone-biles-olympics-gymnastics-withdrawal-twisties/

2. OlympicTalk (October 8, 2023). NBC Sports. Simone Biles closes gymnastics worlds with two more gold medals. Retrieved December 2023 from https://www.nbcsports.com/olympics/news/simone-biles-gymnastics-world-championships-2023-medals. Olympics (October 8, 2023). Artistic Gymnastics World Championships 2023: Simone Biles claims two more golds on final day of competition. The USA gymnast now has 23 career wins at the global meet and 30 overall medals. Retrieved December 2023 from https://olympics.com/en/news/artistic-gymnastics-world-champi onships-2023-apparatus-finals-simone-biles-two-golds-final-day